Praise for *The Seven Keys to Effective Business-to-Business Appointment Setting*

"I have to admit, when I first heard about the idea of a "Blitz" training course, it didn't exactly have me jumping up and down with enthusiasm. The first thing that came to mind was a merciless Teutonic woman cracking a whip and screaming "Call, Call, Call 'till you fall." At the very least, I counted on an illusory gain at best. By making us call a huge volume of prospects, we would generate more leads than usual by sheer force of will.

That was my initial idea of what it would be like. To my delight, I found that I had been wrong in every imagined particular. The pre-call review was spirited and entertaining, as well as driving home the information we needed. The calling sessions were designed to go quickly and pleasantly, giving us the feeling that, while we were doing more, we were doing it in a way that allowed plenty of downtime to rest and recharge. Most of all, however, is the fact that the programs worked. Not only do I feel like I will take the techniques I learned that day with me on all my cold calling activities, but I actually feel that I am now better at my job than I was before your course. I feel I know more about what I need to do and bring more to the table to my job, now and in the future.

Thank you very much for your help and expertise. It is rare that an experience can be both pleasant and so incredibly productive. You've got a fan for life."

-Jeffrey Aronowitz, Account Manager, FineStar Imaging LLC

"Of all the activities a salesperson has to do, cold calling is by far the most challenging. Even the most indomitable salesperson would choose to poke sharp objects into their eyes rather than call complete strangers in an attempt to engage in conversation that, nine times out of ten, turns into utter rejection. But like it or not, cold call prospecting is a must. Successful cold calling requires more than dialing the phone, I have found Andrea Sittig-Rolf's Blitz Experience to be a mostly-painless way to give my team the techniques and preparation to get the most out of customer demand-creation through direct calling. At Datalight, the leader in software for data storage in embedded devices, we have increased our success rate three fold by applying the disciplines taught in The Blitz Experience. I highly recommend it for those companies that want to increase sales opportunities while reducing the frustrations for their sales personnel."

-Dan Prescott, Director of Sales, Datalight Inc.

The Seven Keys to Effective Business-to-Business Appointment Setting

Unlock Your Sales Potential

Andrea Sittig-Rolf

MAT #40687036

ISBN 1-59622-542-4
Library of Congress Control Number: 2006928542

For corrections, updates, comments or any other inquiries please email AspatoreEditorial@thomson.com.

First Printing, 2006
10 9 8 7 6 5 4 3 2 1

Aspatore Books is the largest and most exclusive publisher of C-Level executives (CEO, CFO, CTO, CMO, Partner) from the world's most respected companies and law firms. Aspatore annually publishes a select group of C-Level executives from the Global 1,000, top 250 law firms (Partners and Chairs), and other leading companies of all sizes. C-Level Business Intelligence™, as conceptualized and developed by Aspatore Books, provides professionals of all levels with proven business intelligence from industry insiders—direct and unfiltered insight from those who know it best—as opposed to third-party accounts offered by unknown authors and analysts. Aspatore Books is committed to publishing an innovative line of business and legal books, those which lay forth principles and offer insights that when employed, can have a direct financial impact on the reader's business objectives, whatever they may be. In essence, Aspatore publishes critical tools – need-to-read as opposed to nice-to-read books – for all business professionals

Table of Contents

Foreword

If you, or your sales team, could set a higher number of better and more qualified appointments, would that help your sales career? If you answered yes, then *The Seven Keys to Effective Business-to Business Appointment Setting* is just for you.

Through the years our company has trained thousands of salespeople on how to be more successful in sales and in all areas of life. Success in sales takes the right combination of character, will, and skill. It takes a strong mental "will" to do all of the things necessary to be successful. When you combine motivation and a positive attitude with "will", then activity follows. But that alone is not enough. Add skill and you will get results.

I encourage you to read this book with a highlighter. In fact, one of the tips in the book is to write the techniques you want to implement onto note cards, and put them right next to your phone. But don't stop there. Put them into action.

If you do, amazing things will happen!

One of the greatest benefits of learning a new skill and then putting it into action is the positive impact it has on your attitude. Knowing how to set great appointments will translate into energy and confidence on the phone. Your activity will increase, and because your skill has increased, so will your results.

Does it work? I know it works! You see, not only have we trained thousands of salespeople through the years, we are also a customer of The Blitz Experience, and we have benefited from the skills and techniques taught in this book.

This reminds me of something I heard my father, Zig Ziglar, say at a seminar one time. A customer came up to him with a big grin on his face and said, "Zig, I just bought everything you have, and now I am going to be successful." Dad, looked at him and said, "It will work, if *you* do."

The Seven Keys to Effective Business-to-Business Appointment Setting is in your hands. "It will work, if *you* do."

Tom Ziglar
CEO
Ziglar

Acknowledgments

The purpose of writing this book is to share the successful business-to-business appointment setting techniques that have evolved as a result of practicing them myself and teaching them to other successful sales professionals during my Blitz Experience activity-based sales training program created in May of 2002.

In addition to my siblings Katy, Janet, and Carl, and my husband Brian, who have always been extremely supportive, I want to specifically thank my Blitz Experience clients who have inspired me to write this book.

Thank you for your confidence in choosing to work with me to inspire, motivate, and teach your sales team. Thank you also for your insights into further developing The Blitz Experience program to where it is today!

Introduction

Are you like most sales professionals? Do you do a great job selling to your prospects and customers once you have the opportunity to meet with them face-to-face, but have difficulty scheduling qualified appointments in order to gain the face-to-face opportunity to sell? Do you wish you could sell to more qualified decision-makers? Are you confident that in tweaking your approach in setting the appointment, you could close more business, earn more money, and be a truly exceptional sales professional? If so, then you've come to the right place, because every sale starts with the appointment, and here you will learn how to get the appointment and ultimately get the sale!

Based on my own experience as a sales professional of more than sixteen years and a business owner of more than four years, I would estimate that what you care about most is the end result of your sales activity—the close. Not surprisingly, the very first step in the sales process, getting the appointment, often has the most impact on the last step, closing the sale. Therefore, when analyzing your sales pipeline, you will find a direct correlation between the quality of your appointments and the quantity of your sales.

To share a little of my background that prompted me to write this book, in May of 2002 I founded Sittig Incorporated and created The Blitz Experience, an activity-based sales training program that empowers salespeople to learn and practice business-to-business appointment-setting skills, resulting in a pipeline full of new opportunities at the end of the day. In the last four years of conducting The Blitz Experience, it has become apparent that setting appointments with qualified prospects has everything to do with ultimately closing the sale. If you are in the business of scheduling face-to-face appointments with prospects, you know the importance of getting that first face-to-face meeting to start the sales process.

Think of your best customers. How did the relationships start? What did you do to get the appointment, gain their trust, and close the sale? Throughout the process of working with these customers, did they return your calls, respond to your e-mails, and call you with questions? My guess is yes. Why? What did you do to earn this level of respect from your customers when they were still a prospect? Did you have to "ask for the sale?" My guess is no. The point is that when you take the time to effectively set appointments with qualified prospects and build trust with your prospects, the "close" is not something you have to ask for, but rather something that happens naturally because you used effective appointment-setting techniques right from the beginning.

Rest assured that this book does not cover the same old appointment-setting techniques you will find in every other sales book you've read. Traditional appointment-setting techniques and gimmicks don't work with decision-makers; credibility and results do. Here you will learn innovative selling strategies such as developing a personal introduction from a referral. From generating qualified leads through free online resources to networking with colleagues by asking for specific contacts, this book will explain step by step how you can become an exceptional business-to-business appointment setter. Other unique ideas include practicing the "Aha!" technique when encountering objections from high-level executives (i.e., **A**nticipating the objection, **H**andling the objection, and **A**sking for the appointment). Also, you will get great advice on how to win ambassadors among prospects who will sell for you when you are not there. Finally, this book will explain how to track and understand your personal appointment-setting numbers to better understand the level of activity required in the beginning of the sales process to accomplish your desired outcome and income at the end of the sales process.

This book not only outlines the seven keys to effective business-to-business appointment-setting techniques, but it also includes activities that will help you generate the most qualified opportunities, create trust and credibility with ambassadors and prospects, and ultimately close more business with the kind of clients with whom you would most like to do business.

I encourage you to read the book once in its entirety and then go back and read it again, completing each of the activities presented at the end of each chapter. When you have finished doing that, you will have begun to create the effective appointment-setting habits and strategies that will dramatically improve your sales results and overall income level. Also, if you haven't already, pick up a copy of my first book, *Business-to-Business Prospecting: Innovative Techniques to Get Your Foot in the Door with Any Prospect* (Aspatore Books, 2005), available at Amazon.com and Barnes & Noble bookstores, as it covers many prospecting techniques that will lay the groundwork for the techniques discussed in this book.

I would welcome the opportunity to hear about your results using the appointment-setting techniques offered in this book. Please e-mail me at info@sittiginc.com or call 206-769-4886.

Happy appointment setting!

Andrea Sittig-Rolf
Redmond, Washington

1

Defining Business
Contact Relationships

To begin to understand how to effectively set appointments with qualified decision-makers, we must first define the four levels of business contact relationships. Ultimately, we want to work towards leveraging a specific type of relationship to gain the most effective strategy when setting appointments with qualified decision-makers.

First, while a referral indicates a close professional relationship and the ability to use the name of the person who referred you when contacting a new prospect, a lead is simply information your referral source has shared with you. For example, if I shared information with you about an opportunity to sell your products and services to a client of mine and told you to use my name as a reference when making contact, that is a *referral*. However, if I simply shared the information with you that there was an opportunity to sell your products and services to a client of mine, but I did not allow you to use my name as a reference, that is a *lead*. Obviously, in this case, a referral is better than a lead.

The next level of relationship is what's known as a *personal introduction*. The difference is that while a referral allows you to use the name of the person who referred you, a personal introduction means your referral source is going to make contact with the prospect for you, on your behalf, which is even better than a referral.

What is an ambassador? An ambassador is the best networking partner you'll ever have and the fastest way to set appointments with your most desired prospects. Having an ambassador is like having a salesperson who works just for you, for free! Specifically, an ambassador is someone outside your organization, preferably inside an organization that is a client or who you would like to have as a client, who believes wholeheartedly in you and the product or service you sell. So much so, that as your ambassador, he or she is willing to promote and/or "sell" your product or service among peers and colleagues as well as within his or her own organization.

Now that you understand each of the key business contact relationships, let's take a look at how to further develop leads, referrals, personal introductions, and ambassadors.

For example, let's say you are a commercial office furniture salesperson and you have a lead that ABC Company down the street is moving in several months. Because any company who is moving makes a good lead for you, you will want to explore the best strategy to approach the opportunity. By turning your lead into a referral, you have a much better chance of setting the appointment and developing the sale.

In order to turn your lead into a referral, contact your existing database of networking partners and customers and ask what they know about ABC Company, who is moving in a few months. Chances are, someone in your database will know something about ABC Company or even know someone who works there, and they will be able to refer you to the right person to set the appointment and get your foot in the door. This technique is called "target prospecting" and will be discussed in more detail in key four of this book, "Networking: Leveraging Crucial Relationships to Get Appointments with Qualified Decision-Makers."

Using this same example, when you've discovered someone in your database who knows someone at ABC Company and would be willing to refer you, instead, ask them for a personal introduction. Ask your referral partner to make a phone call on your behalf, or schedule coffee for you and your referral partner's contact to meet in person. Now, instead of simply being referred into ABC Company, you are being personally introduced, which is that much more powerful in terms of getting the appointment and ultimately making the sale.

Finally, the best possible scenario as it relates to business contact relationships, as was discussed at the beginning of this chapter, is winning ambassadors. Although winning ambassadors can take time, the payoff is incredible! The good news is that there is actually a strategy you can implement that will successfully turn those you meet through personal introductions into ambassadors.

In order to effectively develop and win ambassadors, you must be able to communicate that your product or service contains three important criteria. First, it's not enough anymore to simply *save* a client time and money, you must now be able to show that what you offer will actually *make* your client money, increase their revenue, and improve their bottom line. Keep in mind that there are creative ways of showing this if what you sell can't show, in hard dollars, that it will improve your client's bottom line. For example, if you are a printing company, it's pretty tough to show that printing business cards, brochures, and other marketing collateral will make money for your client. But what if the quality of work you do is so much better than that of your competition that you can show that your print job will get noticed more than that of your competition? What if your print job presents a better image for your client than the competition's print job? What if you are able to make recommendations to your client, based on their specific requirements, as to the appropriate paper, ink, formatting, and so on, so that the marketing collateral you print for them is exactly the image they want to portray? Then couldn't you argue that by allowing your client to present a better image up front, based on the quality of work you provide, your client is more likely to get that extra deal or two a year? What is an extra deal or two a year worth, in terms of hard dollars, to your client?

The reason I use this as an example is because I was a client of a local printing company who, I found out later, did *not* make the right recommendations to me in terms of ink, paper, and formatting. As such, I found out about a year later, that the brochure I had been sending in the mail was completely smeared with ink and actually looked dirty by the time my prospect received it! It was only when I was considering using a new printing company for a new brochure that I discovered this. The gentleman I worked with at the new printer asked to see copies of my old brochure so he would have a feel for the type of paper, ink, and other material my project would require; so I mailed him an old brochure. When we met in person to go over my options for the new brochure, he showed me the old brochure I had sent him in the mail. I was horrified to think I'd been sending that brochure in the mail for the past year to so many prospects! The inside of the brochure was black and red ink printed on glossy white paper. Because of the paper and ink combination my previous printer used, the black and red ink had smeared all over the white glossy paper. The ink was dry, but due to the movement of the brochure pages against each other within the envelope, the ink had created smudges all over the inside of the brochure. Needless to say, I never used my previous printing company again. The new printing company I began working with won my current and all future business based on his recommendations of how to improve the smeared ink problem by using a heavier, better-quality paper and a different type of ink that would not smear. Now, I actually receive compliments on my new brochures not only for the design, but for the quality of the paper and crispness of the ink. I'm convinced I will earn that extra deal or two a year based on the first impression I am now presenting when I send out a new brochure as my first point of contact with a new prospect. An extra deal or two a year could be worth tens of thousands of dollars to me, so I conclude that by using this new printing company, I am actually making more money now than I was when I used my old printing company!

The second "ambassador-winning criterion" is that your product or service needs to make your ambassador look good to his or her peers. In other words, the ambassador needs to feel proud that he or she discovered you, as if you are a golden nugget or little-known treasure that only your ambassador found. Meeting this criterion requires that you provide the very best quality product or service in a timely manner and at a reasonable price. You must under-promise and over-deliver in every case when dealing with your ambassador and his or her company. From meeting your ambassador's colleagues for the first time, to managing the project, including offering client service and invoicing, you must consistently provide the best quality work available anywhere in your industry.

The third criterion, if your ambassador prefers it, is to keep him or her apprised of your dealings with his or her company. Your ambassador may or may not want you to do this, so just ask.

I have several ambassadors at each of the organizations I will describe that consistently promote my sales training programs to their peers, colleagues, and channel partners. One of them is a marketing firm that actually builds my program into the marketing plans they provide for their clients. Another ambassador, who is the president of a commercial furniture manufacturing rep firm, asked me to create a PowerPoint presentation for him to present to his industry manufacturing companies and dealer network in an effort to promote my Blitz programs. I also have ambassadors at a Fortune 11, multibillion-dollar technology company who promote my Blitz programs to their partner dealers. My client is already sold on the concept of The Blitz Experience and the results it creates for them and their partners, so not only do they endorse and recommend the Blitz program to their partner dealers, but they sponsor it too. In other words, my client pays for the investment for their partner dealers to participate. By operating this way, not only do my client's partner dealers benefit from the training, my client benefits due to the increase in their products sold through their partner dealers. Here is an example of an actual e-mail I received that my ambassadors at this company send to their partner dealers promoting the Blitz program:

"Hi, John. As we talked about yesterday, we have an exciting new way for you to spend your marketing funds! I'd like to introduce you to Andrea Sittig-Rolf, a.k.a. the Blitz Master. She is the creator of The Blitz Experience, an activity-based sales training program that empowers salespeople to hone their telephone prospecting skills. Her program is unique, because it requires salespeople to actually call real prospects to generate leads and schedule appointments the day of the training. The Blitz is a "learning laboratory." It is a combination of learning and practicing the skills around getting past gatekeepers, overcoming common objections, getting the appointment, and leaving effective voicemail messages that get returned. It is a one-day program beginning at 8:30 a.m. and wrapping up around 4:00 p.m. and includes four hours of telephone time. A team of ten salespeople, on average, will schedule anywhere between forty-five and seventy-five appointments (or leads) and will close anywhere between

$100,000 to $250,000 in business within ninety days of the program as a direct result of the appointments scheduled and leads generated during the Blitz! For more information about this one-of-a-kind sales training program, please visit www.sittiginc.com or contact Andrea Sittig-Rolf at 206-769-4886 or andrea@sittiginc.com. Thank you!"

Then, the note below this e-mail I received from my ambassador says:

"Andrea, I spoke with John about your services and success you are having with our various partners. He is interested in learning more from you and what you can offer his company and sales staff."

Does it get any better than this?

Furthermore, a local regionally based insurance company who has been a Blitz Experience client on the direct sales side is now promoting it to their community agency sales teams as a way to increase their market share within the agency community as well as a way to help the community agents sell more by offering them effective sales training. My ambassador at this client is actually setting up appointments for us to go on together to present The Blitz Experience to his community agent insurance groups. Once we arrive and he introduces me to the community insurance agency president, my ambassador has done such a good job promoting the Blitz that it's pretty much just a matter of selecting a date on the calendar for their Blitz!

Finally, I have created an ambassador out of each of the executive vice presidents of a client in the banking industry, focusing on their multi-family and commercial mortgage lending divisions, who continue to promote The Blitz Experience to others in the organization, allowing me deeper and broader access into that particular account.

Without exception, I've shown each of my ambassadors how my sales training offering will make them money and make them look good. I also keep them apprised of my dealings with those they have recommended to me. Now that this ambassador network has been established, it continues to grow exponentially, and I find myself doing less marketing and more delivering of my programs, resulting in the hiring of two new employees to meet the demand my ambassador network has created. My company has become more profitable, because I am spending less time and energy marketing my Blitz programs and looking for new clients and more time doing the work I love and get paid for, which is implementing my Blitz programs!

Ambassadors are the cheapest sales team you will ever find. You don't have to pay them a salary. You don't even have to pay them a commission or bonus, and you don't have to offer any extravagant incentives, although it is nice to appreciate your ambassadors as much as you can by taking them to lunch every now and then and remembering them during the holidays! This model of leveraging ambassadors for setting appointments and going to market is extremely effective and valuable when you consider the time and money you will save in finding new clients. Just find a few ambassadors and let them seek and find your new clients for you!

Finally, it is important that you develop more than one ambassador at each prospect or customer organization. Often, your ambassador will leave the company you're working with and go somewhere else. In many cases, this is a good thing if the ambassador continues to sing your praises at the new company and brings you in as a vendor. However, unless you have developed more than one ambassador at the original company, you may have to start over in terms of developing business at that company. If, however, you developed more than one ambassador at that company and one ambassador leaves to go somewhere else, you're still covered by the ambassadors remaining at that company.

Recently, one of my ambassadors from a commercial office furniture manufacturing firm in Seattle, Washington, took a job with a Fortune 20 global financial services company in Hartford, Connecticut. Remembering the fantastic results her sales team had when she was with the commercial office furniture manufacturing firm, she called me to request a proposal for a Blitz program for her new team at the financial services company. This has become the largest global opportunity for Sittig Incorporated since starting the business four years ago!

ACTIVITY:

Choose one contact at your best customer and use the approach explained above to turn him or her into an ambassador. Repeat until you have a plethora of ambassadors. Leverage these relationships to schedule appointments with key decision-makers for new opportunities within your customer's organization.

2

Asking for Help

Why reinvent the appointment-setting wheel, so to speak? Because I wholeheartedly believe in learning from others whom I consider experts, I wanted to share with you some of the best appointment-setting skills and strategies I received from generous sales professionals in my network who were willing to contribute material to this book.

Starting at the top, I asked several of my clients who are the decision-makers at their firms, "How do you like to be approached by salespeople on the phone? What resonates with you in terms of granting the first appointment to the salesperson when they call?" Some general themes run through their answers such as building rapport, follow-through, and third-party referrals. Here's what else they had to say:

Flavio Veiga, president of Circulo dos Profissionais de Vendas in Brazil, shared the following story with me. A salesperson from a Web designer firm called him and asked if he would be willing to answer two simple questions and said, "What do you like the most about your current site?" After his answer, she claimed to understand, and then asked, "What would you like to see improved in it?" After this second answer, she went for the kill and said, "I believe we can achieve that if we work together with you. What is the most convenient date for us to visit?" Flavio's objection was, "You need to see Baggio, the man who takes care of that, not me." The salesperson then said, "Yes, sir, I already talked to Mr. Baggio, and asked him if I could try to have you present at our meeting this Friday. That's why I'm calling you, sir. We have found that the results are much better if we get the president involved at the start. Is that all right with you, sir?" Flavio granted her the meeting, because she was prepared when she made the call to him by previously speaking with his partner.

Another contact of mine who is the vice president of North American sales for an enterprise software company shared that she always grants appointments to salespeople who call her who are referred or are reps she met in person at a conference or other event. She also shared that she grants meetings to salespeople who are interested in an "informational interview." The informational interview suggests meeting just to learn more about each other's businesses rather than meeting in a buy-and-sell scenario. This same contact is also impressed by those who use a clever approach to connect with her. She shared an example of a salesperson who found out who her favorite college team was and then sent her tickets to a game. While she was unable to accept the tickets, she did thank the salesperson for his creativity and scheduled a follow-up appointment.

Lauriann Reynolds, a stellar high-level sales professional in the insurance business, had this to say. "Use a network. Get a third-party reference to introduce you whenever possible. Use third-party testimonials." She shared a fantastic story about a salesperson who followed this very approach just the other day. Apparently, an expert in audio/visual and event planning who does not currently do business with her company arranged for someone with whom she had worked to get the three of them together for a "lunch chat." They built rapport and left the lunch with the beginning of a relationship. The salesperson didn't try to ask for the business or go for the close. Instead, they talked about their families, his ideas on event planning, and so on. Of course, Lauriann shared, the important next step is the follow-through, the key ingredient, in her mind, to solidifying the business.

Lauriann also shared with me that she appreciates receiving value-added information from salespeople. Her advice to salespeople is rather than sending marketing material to your clients, send them something of value. For example, an interesting article from the newspaper, a handout, or anything that may be of interest to the client that's not your company's collateral.

Roy Sherrill, president and chief executive officer of Datalight, a data in embedded devices technology company located in Bothell, Washington, says he is turned off by salespeople who call about what they want or what they want to do. He is more interested in meeting with salespeople who can sell him on a benefit and not on a product or service. He suggests writing a fifteen- to thirty-second pitch that sells a benefit with enough hooks that make him want to meet in person.

In addition to this, winning salespeople I've worked with over the years were generous enough to include their ideas and thoughts on business-to-business appointment setting and what has worked for them. Getting past the gatekeeper is a common theme.

Elizabeth Morgan, a successful new business development professional with an architect firm in Seattle, Washington, shares her philosophy of starting at the top when contacting a new prospect. She includes the gatekeeper in her process, knowing the gatekeeper is often the administrative assistant to her high-level contacts. Elizabeth has a frank discussion with the receptionist/administrative assistant about why she is calling. Her pitch is simple and honest. She asks for a modest amount of time to learn more about the prospect and their objectives, and to share the differentials of her firm versus other firms they may be considering for their project. Elizabeth's honest approach usually gets her more than an hour with the decision-maker once she's in the door.

Terri Dunevant, licensed provider of The Blitz Experience and president of WinCourage, suggests systematically building a "staircase call list." She shares the following: "Upon signing up an existing client, I asked if she was a member of any association within their industry. To my delight, she proclaimed that as a matter of fact, she was the president of the local chapter! Next, I found out the details of vendor participation within her association and garnered an invitation to their next meeting. At the meeting, their president introduced me, giving me immediate credibility with the audience. Quickly I was able to make several appointments just by calling the following day and stating, "I'm the new vendor you met yesterday. I'd like to meet with you to share what my company has done for the president of your organization, how's Tuesday at 10:00am?" It got me the appointment! Subsequently, I visited other chapters of that organization and applied the same technique, introducing myself as being referred by another chapter and acquiring the president of that chapter as a customer first. Again, many of the other members of that chapter would grant the appointment just to find out what their president found as valuable. Now, I no longer need to visit first. I can call other businesses within that association nationwide, name drop other chapter president clients, and close over the phone."

Arnie Goldstein, licensed provider of The Blitz Experience and an associate of Puget Sound Training Associates, shares the following: "It has been said that, when prospecting, one shouldn't make any assumptions based on past knowledge of a company. I almost fell into that trap recently when calling on a copier dealer I saw in the yellow pages. While I didn't know this dealer personally, I knew that most of their branches had recently been sold off to a manufacturer. I was looking to sell them sales training services and thought they would not be an ideal prospect because the remaining office was small. I called them anyway figuring "the harder you work the luckier you get". The owner said he liked my persistence and agreed to meet me. During our meeting he told me he like my style, appreciated my efforts and valued my references. I also gave him some industry news he did not know about. As it turned out, he had spun off one of his branches and the new company was in a major market. He recommended his former partner to me and I now had a reference from Mr. Big himself to talk with the president of a large dealership. I presented my products and he liked what he heard. It seems he needed exactly what I was offering. I sent them a proposal, he checked my references, and I sold my sales training services to a company I didn't even know existed, all in a matter of two weeks! I learned that if I am to assume anything it should be that I am of value in some way to everyone."

Todd Reeves, a portfolio manager, concurs by saying the first sale is winning the favor of the gatekeeper. Mike Powell, a sales professional with a business intelligence firm in Canada, agrees by saying he always takes a genuine interest in whomever he speaks with from the receptionist to the CEO and everyone in between.

Several salespeople I interviewed had some great suggestions on keeping it short when asking for the initial appointment. Mike Sullivan is the regional director of Passport Unlimited, the first dining program targeted at business professionals offering significant discounts and repeat visits at participating upscale restaurants. Here's what he had to say: "I tend to keep the details about what I want to present to my prospect to a minimum. Too many details and information can give them a reason to say 'No' without giving me the advantage of sitting in front of them, which allows me to read their reaction and adjust."

Terriann Muller, a performance consultant with Zig Ziglar True Performance, makes one more call at the end of the day. If that call does not result in a contact, she hits redial first thing the next morning and most of the time makes the contact and gets the appointment. Brilliant!

Kelley Sieger, a business development professional with Sudden Impact Marketing, says to first do some homework on the company you're planning to call. She also suggests sending a personalized letter or package that will get their attention and says you will be calling at a specific date and time, and then do it. She also recommends getting the name of the administrator or assistant of the prospect you are calling and include in the postscript of your letter that if the date and time you've said you will call is inconvenient, please leave word with the administrator or assistant for a better time to reach the prospect. If you don't have any luck reaching the prospect using this technique, Kelley says to send an e-mail stating that you're sorry you missed them and specify a meeting time and ask them to confirm, deny, or suggest a better time to meet. It takes tenacity, but call again at the designated time. If you still do not reach the prospect, send another brief e-mail and follow up with a phone call. Kelley says it's a process.

Kelley also suggests having a conversation about business issues rather than doing a "product dump." You need to understand your audience and be prepared. She has a great idea for starting the conversation with your prospect, and it goes like this. "Most executives at your level deal with similar business issues. One of the most frequent we hear about is adaptability, that is, responding to the many changes that get thrown at them frequently and in many forms. What issue will be getting most of your attention over the next six to twelve months?" Once they respond, say, "I know the XYZ services team has dealt with similar issues with some of their other clients. A fifteen-minute meeting with your local XYZ representative will quickly determine if there is a basis for a business partnership. They will come in to get a top-level understanding of what issues are most critical to you, and if you decide you like each other, they can do a full-blown discovery and ultimately make some recommendations that could help you. (Restate whatever their critical business issue is.) How about Wednesday at 10:00 a.m.?" Kelley says it's really a variety of doing the numbers, improving your skills, being prepared, knowing your audience, multiple touches, and being able to talk their talk.

Furthermore, Rendi Bell, an account executive with a well-known shipping firm, says, "The best way to overcome the humdrum answers from people who really don't know what they want is to have a new or revised program that will better suit them and entice them with a snippet - just enough to get the appointment."

Also, Ray Mannello, the national account manager for Sprague Pest Solutions, shared an interesting story with me. Not too long ago, he was looking at a year-end report for a major national company and saw the chief executive officer's name and decided to call. He got right through to the chief executive officer and had a nice conversation. His lesson learned from this was that sometimes you just have to make the call right then and there rather than putting it off. He also has some great suggestions when prospects say they are happy with who they're currently using or not interested in meeting. To these objections, Ray says, "I understand your position, and what I've found is that when leaders in your industry such as yourself allow me to come in and meet in person, we can provide at least three options:

1) Validate the current service you have in place.
2) Show you other options that may enhance your current service. These might be options your current provider does not have the capability to provide or options not in their portfolio.
3) Finally, we may show you that there is more value to be had by making a change. You win in all three cases, because you have validated your choices."

In addition to this, Mark Meyer, director of business development for Meridian Technology Group Inc., says a technique he has used and observed is to act incredulous to the prospect when he says he hasn't heard of your company before. It's gutsy, because you don't want to come off as arrogant or seeming like you're bragging, but you still want to be sincere in helping the prospect solve a particular problem. Typically, it would go something like this: "Ms. Jane Doe, I can't believe you haven't heard of us before! We have been in business in the Pacific Northwest since 1990 and have served clients such as Nike, Weyerhaeuser, Microsoft, Getty Images, and more. They have found our services to be very adapted and directed to their needs, thus easing their processes. I would like just fifteen minutes of your time to discuss how we can apply our methodology to your organization. Would Tuesday at 10:00 a.m. work?"

Several of those I interviewed shared some clever ideas to get the first appointment. Cynthia Calhoun, an agent with AFLAC, shared a cute story. On one of her prospecting calls, she began chatting with the woman who answered the phone. The woman was very friendly, and in the course of the conversation Cynthia told her about AFLAC's little plush ducks that quack "AFLAC," and she made the duck "talk" for the woman over the phone. Cynthia told the woman that if she would get Cynthia an appointment with the business owner, she would give her a duck. The woman's response was, "Well, I'm his wife, and I want a duck, so he'll see you. Call back in thirty minutes." When Cynthia called back in thirty minutes, she was put through to the business owner, and he said, "Okay, I'll give you the appointment, but it'll cost you two ducks. My daughter wants one, too!" They've been Cynthia's clients for years now, and over the years she's given them quite a few of the varieties of AFLAC ducks. This is a great story about using what you have, being creative, and having fun to get the business!

John Donnelly, the director of field sales for a supply company in Marietta, Georgia, had this to say: "Send a letter with a sharpened company pencil in the envelope. The letter should state that you will be contacting the prospect before it needs to be re-sharpened." He also says, "Send an introductory letter with a cut-in-half company $50 credit certificate to unopened accounts. In the body of the letter, state that you'll be glad to provide the other half when you personally meet at the initial appointment." And finally, John shares, "If it's a particularly tough customer, write on the back of your business card, 'I can talk to God every day, why can't I talk to you now?'" and mail it. This is good stuff. Thanks, John!

Eric van der Horst of basiX says if the prospect recognizes he or she has a problem, never say you have a solution. Instead, ask first what the financial impact is of the problem to the company. Financial impacts are typically what prospects are most concerned about, so if you can get them to identify and quantify the financial impact, you have something to work towards in preparing for your meeting.

Jay Trinidad, a communications specialist with a Seattle-based telecommunications firm, keeps it simple by saying, "Learn what matters." In other words, don't go on and on with your agenda, because it may mean nothing to your prospect. Instead, learn what matters to your prospects and tailor your pitch accordingly. Jay also suggests getting to the office early, which is when you will most often reach decision-makers.

A business development professional for a general contractor in Bellevue, Washington, says he has had success name-dropping some of his "blue ribbon" clients and giving a word or two about what he's doing with them currently or referencing past projects he's worked on with them. He also talks about the big picture in the industry, including market trends and the like. His goal is to introduce himself and his company and learn more about the prospect's goals and upcoming projects they may be planning. He wants to convey the message that he's looking at an extended window of potentially working together and is not expecting anything immediately. He's just trying to connect two good firms to see if there is the possibility of a connection. He wants to get to know them, and he wants that to come across genuinely.

Finally, Sarah Taylor, motivational speaker and author of *Secrets of Pharmaceutical Salespeople* (Sarah A. Taylor, 2004), shares her best technique of getting face time with her prospects. She often attends her prospect's industry's largest convention, where they will be exhibiting to their customers. She goes to their exhibit booths and tells a salesperson or manager what she does. She confidently asks them to introduce her to the vice president of sales or whoever she would need to talk to about her services. She has found the people in exhibit booths to be so helpful, and by the time they introduce her to the executive, she's practically a friend and is introduced as such! Almost every large order she has received for her books, as well as her training sessions, has come through using this approach.

I want to thank those of you who contributed these very important keys to success when setting appointments with qualified prospects. Thanks for allowing my readers the luxury of not having to reinvent the appointment-setting wheel and learning from your success!

In addition to the generous support of my contacts, I also want to highly recommend an important resource for anyone in the sales and marketing profession. Sales and Marketing Executives International (SMEI) is the worldwide nonprofit professional association serving the sales and marketing community. Founded in 1935 and with over 10,000 members around the world, SMEI is focused on its "Five Founding Principles":

1) Professional identification and standards
2) Continuing education
3) Sharing knowledge
4) Assisting students
5) Supporting free enterprise

SMEI is the only worldwide knowledge growth and relationship-building forum created for sales and marketing executives. Since no other worldwide executive sales and marketing associations exist, SMEI fills a void by providing a personal and professional community devoted to providing knowledge, growth, leadership, and connections between peers in both sales and marketing. With over fifty affiliate chapters around the world, members benefit from both the strength of an international organization and the resources a local chapter provides through ongoing seminars, lectures, and networking opportunities. Find SMEI online at www.smei.org.

In addition to SMEI, another important resource for continuing your sales education is SalesRepRadio.com. SalesRepRadio is a fantastic resource for continuing education for the savvy sales professional. SalesRepRadio has two components. The first is SalesRepRadio To-Go, a monthly audio magazine designed exclusively for sales reps and sales managers. Available on CD or instant MP3 download, it's loaded with timely sales advice from North America's top sales training professionals. That's right, the same experts your company pays thousands to for live training are brought together every month on one disc for an informative, educational, and motivational talk radio-style interview.

The second component to SalesRepRadio is the Web site www.salesrepradio.com, which is an excellent resource for the latest and greatest in sales techniques with new sales experts featured each week.

ACTIVITY:

Identify the decision-makers at your top three prospects and use the techniques described here to get the appointment.

3

Preparing to Schedule Appointments

Have you ever had clients who were more trouble than they were worth? Often, we're so anxious to close the deal that we don't think about whether we really want that particular client. My guess is, however, that for the clients who turn out to be more trouble than they're worth, you had some inkling or gut feeling about them right from the beginning of the sales process. You had intuition that it might be a "high-maintenance" client or, worse, a "nightmare client"; but for whatever reason, you didn't pay attention to your inner voice. The fact is that we're better off saying "No" to such an opportunity than taking it, based on the hardship and energy drain it may cost in the long run. Before you can even begin to schedule your appointments, you must first know with whom your appointments should be scheduled.

The financial services industry has figured out that creating an ideal client profile (ICP) is the key to success in their business, and I think we should all follow their lead. Not only do financial advisors use the ICP as a tool to help them determine their best clients, but they use it as a tool to help their prospects determine that they might, in fact, be an ideal client for the financial advisor. The financial advisor's ICP is even worded in such a way that anyone reading it would like to think of themselves as an ideal client for that financial advisor. In other words, the stated ICP is appealing to prospective clients because it uses flattering terminology. Below is an excerpt from one financial services company ICP I found on the Internet:

> At Canterbury Financial Group, we serve successful individuals who expect excellence and have made a firm

commitment to achieving it themselves. In general, the people who benefit most from our services tend to fit the following description:

Recognize the connection between accumulated assets and
the freedom to pursue their life vision
Successful in their careers
Respected in the community
Involved in rewarding activities or still employed
Friendly, helpful, open-minded
Consider managing money a burden, not a hobby

Our Clients:

- Share in the realization that the freedom to pursue their compelling life vision is linked to their accumulated assets
- Want to simplify their lives and are willing to enter into a mutually beneficial long-term relationship with a personal wealth manager
- Are highly motivated to work with a fee-only adviser who knows them personally and has only their best interests in mind

(Canterbury Financial Group ICP found online at www.canterburygroup.com/idealclient)

I don't know about you, but after reading this company's ICP, it makes me want to sign up! So, not only does the ICP serve as a tool for you to target your prospecting activities, but it can also serve as a marketing tool to your prospects who will want to be considered your ideal client.

Imagine if you had such a tool for your prospects to use to then tell you they would like to be your next ideal client. How powerful would such a tool be to leverage in your marketing materials and prospecting activities? In this chapter, I will cover how to create your ICP and then use it as a powerful business-to-business appointment-setting tool. I will also offer solid advice on finding online resources for sales information in order to better understand your prospect before calling to schedule the appointment.

How many times have you actually thought about who your ideal client is, versus finding the next person who you think is just willing to buy from you? Think about it. Think about how your business would change if it was made up of "ideal clients." Think about an ideal client you currently work with. What makes them ideal? What are the parameters of, or formula for, your ideal client? What size company are they? How many employees do they have? How much do they do in revenue each year? Who are their clients? What is their product or service? How many locations do they have? How do they go to market (i.e., direct versus indirect sales, retail, channel sales, etc.)? How much revenue do you do each year with your ideal client? Do you do repeat business with your ideal client? How many decision-makers must you deal with to get a "Yes" in working with your ideal client? How much client service is involved in working with your ideal client? Does your ideal client give you referrals to other ideal clients? These are all questions that should be considered when defining your ICP. They will also lead to certain industries or specific vertical markets that will make excellent prospects for you based on the nature of their industry or business, as identified in your ICP.

In defining your ICP, you can begin to focus only on those clients who fit your ICP. This also allows you to quickly identify someone who is *not* an ideal client and move on to someone who is. Think about how much more effective you could be in attracting ideal clients when you're no longer wasting time with prospects who aren't the best fit for what you sell anyway, for whatever reason. It took me two years after starting my business to realize the difference between ideal clients and non-ideal clients. When I first started the company and began promoting The Blitz Experience, I initially focused on any company, no matter what size, that had a sales team of at least three people. Without knowing it, that is how I was defining my ICP: companies who had a sales team of at least three people. That's it—no other factors were taken into consideration. This approach forced me to "start over" not only each month, but literally each day to determine where my next paycheck was coming from, since there was often no potential for any future business with that client. And believe me, that's no way to live! I was successful at finding clients, but I was running myself ragged because they were mostly small, one-time clients.

Two years after starting my business, I stumbled onto an account that had a large sales team in the form of a "dealer network." It was a commercial furniture manufacturing company that went to market not through a direct sales channel, but through manufacture rep companies and dealers across the country who sold their products to the end user. Lo and behold, I had hit the mother lode and didn't even know it! It started small, with a Blitz Experience program here and there, but soon word got out and I actually had to hire other "Blitz Masters" (sales trainers) just to meet the demand that was created for the program within their dealer network! The next client I landed had a similar profile, except they were a major software manufacturing company. They too went to market not through a direct sales channel, but through a dealer network. Similar to the commercial furnishings company, this client began with two Blitz Experience programs with a dealer in North Carolina, and when the program was so successful at that location, I received an e-mail from the general manager telling me he wanted to roll out the program to the remaining 300 sales reps in eight other cities! That single project generated more revenue for my company than all of the revenue generated in the previous two years combined!

Finally, after two years, I had begun to get the hang of it. I got to thinking, "Hmmm, what is it about these two clients that is so different from the other clients I have been working with?" That's when I decided to create a formal process to determine my ICP. First, by defining the ideal client and then pursuing only those prospects that fit the ICP, I would have an entire business focused on only the best of the best. I would also learn to quickly identify who fit the ICP and who did not so I could move on quickly in situations where a prospect was not ideal according to the profile. I thought, "Why not turn the tables on this whole sales game? Why does it have to be that the client gets to choose whether to work with my company? Why can't I choose which clients I want to work with?" I actually increased my revenue by eight and a half times my average just by deciding what it was about these two new accounts that made them so lucrative for my business.

What came next, after defining my ICP, was the realization that by nature of certain industries, there was an automatic fit with my ICP. For example, I soon realized that commercial office furniture and software manufacturing companies were both excellent vertical markets because of the way they went to market through dealer networks, indicating that the same type of opportunity existed because of these particular industries and the way they traditionally go to market. After selecting other commercial office furniture and software manufacturing companies, the only other determining factor was their size. If they were a small manufacturing company and only had a handful of dealers, it was not something I would pursue. However, if they were a large company with an extensive dealer network, it was something I would pursue.

I also soon realized that large companies who sold directly to their clients, rather than going through a sales channel methodology, were great prospects for The Blitz Experience. It made sense to pilot the program at one office and then, with proven success, roll it out to the entire company. This tactic allowed me to sell the program just once to the key decision-makers at large organizations and then simply fulfill Blitz orders once the word spread and salespeople as well as sales managers in the organization began to hear about the success of the Blitz program in other departments.

Now that you understand the importance of creating your ICP before making your appointment-setting calls, let's review next how to find key online resources to keep your pipeline full of qualified leads.

Some invaluable resources I have found online for lead generation include Google Alerts (www.googlealerts.com) and Biz Journal Search Watches (www.bizjournals.com/account/register), as well as Web sites such as www.hoovers.com, www.sellingpower.com, www.salesandmarketing.com, www.lead411.com, www.linkedin.com, and www.justsell.com.

Let's review each of these fantastic resources. Google Alerts are e-mail updates of the latest relevant Google results (Web, news, etc.) based on your choice of query or topic. Google Alerts allow you to automatically receive information related to prospects, customers, competitors, and other information to help generate qualified leads and drive new business. Some handy uses of Google Alerts include:
- Monitoring a developing news story
- Keeping current on a competitor or industry

- Getting the latest on a celebrity or event
- Keeping tabs on your favorite sports teams

Think about trigger events in your industry that could be used as Google Alerts. Is the hiring of a specific type of personnel something that would be a trigger event for a lead in your industry? What about a company that is moving or has moved? Are mergers and acquisitions good leads for you? All of these instances can be created as a Google Alert and notify you on a regular basis about the goings-on in the marketplace and can be a constant source of leads for you.

In my business, for example, it is important to know which companies have a vice president of sales, since they are typically the decision-maker in regards to sales training, and a vice president level indicates a certain size company that would fit my ICP. Also, strategic alliances indicate the "dealer network" format that fits my ICP. I receive press release e-mails each day from Google that contain the words "vice president of sales" and "strategic alliance." Since the press release usually has to do with the hiring or promotion of a vice president of sales or the forming of a new strategic alliance, that tells me the particular company is growing and has budget available in their sales department. It also gives me the name of my contact, the vice president of sales, or the person in charge of the strategic alliance.

Biz Journals Search Watches are also a fantastic resource. Go to www.bizjournals.com/account/register. You can create a Biz Journals Search Watch by first registering and creating an account. This is a free service that will track your customers, prospects, and competitors, and then e-mail you when they appear in one of Biz Journals' articles. This service becomes a powerful tool that allows you to stay on top of the latest business news without having to do all the research yourself. You can create as many Search Watches as you like.

Hoover's is an online business information resource that gives all kinds of information about a particular company or even a particular executive. It does the research for you and is a great tool to use when measuring a lead against your ICP. It even allows you to create prospect lists based on your ICP. Check it out at www.hoovers.com.

Once you've determined some of the pertinent information by using Google Alerts and Biz Journals Search Watches, before calling on the prospects you find, do some research on Hoover's and on the company website to understand more about the prospect's business, such as the number of employees, number of locations, and annual revenue. Once you determine that the lead fits your ICP, you now have a reason to call the prospect.

Sometimes, it's necessary to play detective and use a combination of the above-mentioned resources to find the information you need. Let's say, for example, you have searched for a type of company in Google and found several websites that meet your search criteria. In researching the various companies you found through Google, you are unable to find the name of the appropriate contact. Once you have the name of the company for which you would like to have the appropriate contact name, you can then enter the company name in Hoover's to find the appropriate contact within the company.

SellingPower.com and *SellingPower* magazine satisfy the information needs of business-to-business sales managers and serve the sales professionals market with a circulation greater than any other sales magazine. Its readers subscribe to *SellingPower* to learn more about effective sales and marketing techniques to improve the development of their own businesses. It is a great resource to further your education in sales and to keep you apprised of the latest and greatest sales techniques and methodologies. SellingPower can be found online at www.sellingpower.com.

Sales & Marketing Management is the leading authority for executives in the sales and marketing field. In every issue of the magazine, and on their website, readers have easy access to the most relevant trends, strategies, exclusive research, expert voices, and cutting-edge case studies designed to help them sell more, manage better, and market smarter. Check it out at www.salesandmarketing.com.

Lead 411 provides an online sales leads service and database that delivers daily leads from news, company profiles, business e-mail lists, and executive mailing lists. The technology and manual research ensures quality information and hours of saved time. Use the lead generation techniques to boost your prospecting. Lead 411 is on the Web at www.lead411.com.

LinkedIn is an online network of more than 5.5 million experienced professionals from around the world, representing 130 industries. When you join, you create a profile that summarizes your professional accomplishments. Your profile helps you find and be found by former colleagues, clients, and partners. You can add more connections by inviting trusted contacts to join LinkedIn and connect to you. Your network consists of your connections, your connections' connections, and the people they know, linking you to thousands of qualified professionals.

LinkedIn is an amazing tool. Through your network you can:

- Find potential clients, service providers, subject experts, and partners who come recommended
- Be found for business opportunities
- Search for great sales jobs
- Discover inside connections that can help you land jobs and close deals
- Get introduced to other professionals through the people you know

And the best part? It's free to join! Find LinkedIn at www.linkedin.com.

Finally, Justsell.com® is another truly invaluable resource if you are a sales professional. It is the Web's resource for sales and marketing leaders. It provides its subscribers and users with free, just-published sales leads, articles, templates, checklists, guides, and discussion forums. Those who will find the most value from the network are:

- Sales managers
- Sales executives
- Sales professionals
- Marketing managers
- Marketing professionals
- Business owners
- Entrepreneurs

- People new to sales management or to the sales profession
- People considering a career change to sales

Each month, this site hones in on a particular piece of the sales process or the sales career and publishes articles and tools by some of the best sales and marketing minds in the country. Those who wish to become an active part of the community can receive a variety of free e-mail newsletters and/or submit their own sales or marketing articles for publication consideration. Find it online at www.justsell.com.

Once you have found great leads using the above-mentioned resources, be sure to conduct the appropriate research before contacting the prospect in order to sound educated on the prospect's business during that first important conversation leading up to the appointment. Keep in mind that there is such a thing as "too much research," meaning you use research as an excuse not to get on the phone and make the calls you know you need to make! Try not to spend more than about five minutes researching each lead. Remember, your purpose in the first phone call is to just get the appointment; you will have the opportunity to "sell" later when you meet with the prospect face to face.

One last lead generation technique I'll share is one I discovered by accident. Recently, I was in Louisville, Kentucky, tagging along on a business trip with my husband. While he participated in workshops at the conference he was attending, I hung out in the lobby of the hotel and worked on this book. One day, while typing away on my laptop, I overhead a conversation between a couple of salespeople who were attending a sales conference of a high-tech company. They were salespeople for a major software company that was a channel partner of the company sponsoring the event. I decided to make small talk. After chatting for a few minutes, one of the salespeople asked me what I did for a living. I explained that I created The Blitz Experience activity-based sales training program designed to empower salespeople to schedule appointments with qualified prospects the day of the training, resulting in a pipeline full of new opportunities at the end of the day. As it turns out, the salesperson I was talking to was often involved in "national call-out days" put on by his company to introduce the latest version of their software to the market. He was excited about what I was telling him about The Blitz Experience and said that, as a salesperson, he would appreciate any guidance on how to be more effective when scheduling appointments with new prospects when introducing the newest version of his software. We exchanged business cards and when I returned home from the trip, I sent him some information about The Blitz Experience to share with the executives at his company. After receiving the information I sent, we exchanged e-mail a few times and then, lo and behold, I received an e-mail from the assistant of the vice president of marketing asking me for a meeting to discuss how I could help them make their national call-out days more effective! The moral of the story and this non-traditional lead generation technique? Hang out in hotel lobbies where conferences relative to your business are being held, and strike up a conversation with the people there!

ACTIVITY:

Go to www.googlealerts.com. Create a Google Alert by clicking the "Sign Up" button and then reading the instructions and completing the information in the box to the right of the screen. Consider any "trigger events," for example, companies that are moving, have recently received funding, or are hiring. Then type in the appropriate key words relevant to your business for the topic you wish to monitor. You can create as many Google Alerts on as many different topics as you like. This is an excellent way to generate leads.

4

Networking

etworking for leads is a common way of finding new business. We go to an event, give our business cards to everyone we meet, and hope the exchange will turn into some business. I have a couple of thoughts about networking that may seem a bit outside the norm, but consider this: When networking and asking for leads, first, GIVE a lead—what I like to call "bestow networking." Begin the conversation by focusing on the other person. Ask questions about their business, what makes a good lead for them, and be specific. Consider questions you pose in your ICP, and ask the same of those for whom you might be able to help find leads. What industry are they targeting? What size companies are they looking to work with? What is the title of the person they usually deal with, and so on. As you're gathering this information, think of the people you know in your database of contacts that fit their ICP. You'll be amazed to see what will happen next after you've given a qualified lead or contact based on the answers to the specific questions you've asked. Chances are, you'll walk away with a few good leads too, as long as you're specific in telling the other person what makes a good lead for you, considering your ICP of course.

While I have many stories I could share as examples of the effectiveness of this strategy, I'll share just three. The first happened several years ago when I was meeting with a local research company that was a prospect for my Blitz Experience sales training program. When I arrived and met my contact for the first time, the first words out of his mouth were, "I only have about ten minutes." After building rapport for a few minutes, I began asking questions about his business, mostly relating to their prospecting efforts to determine whether there was truly an opportunity for The Blitz Experience. The best question I asked was, "What makes a good lead for you?" After listening intently and taking a few notes, I realized I had several ideal contacts for him that I was able to share on the spot. By offering a couple of good leads for him, he immediately dropped his guard and suddenly found another hour and a half to spend with me in spite of only having "ten minutes" to talk at the beginning of our meeting! Not only did he give me some great ideas for a new keynote program I was putting together, but he also offered me several great leads!

Another great example of how well "bestow networking" works happened just recently. Kip, a colleague of mine, owns an online commercial real estate listing company that features comprehensive market coverage with listings of buildings, spaces, and subleases available from specific landlords and leasing agents. He sells subscriptions to service-oriented companies that sell to the commercial real estate industry. I personally introduced him to three business owner colleagues of mine and sang the praises of his service, encouraging them to consider signing up. Kip was thrilled to not only have three qualified leads, but personal introductions as well. Later, I wanted to get my foot in the door with a local broadband company and, as it turns out, the president of the company was Kip's cousin. I called Kip to ask for a personal introduction, and he was more than happy to provide it!

Finally, keep in mind that networking doesn't always have to be about exchanging leads to sell the products and services you provide. It can also be a great way to find a job. Recently, a colleague of mine was laid off from a sales position with an information and printing solutions company. She invited me to lunch to talk about the next steps in her career and was hoping I could help her with making contact with potential employers. As it turned out, I did know several companies looking to hire new salespeople at the time, so I made several introductions to position her with the right people in each of the companies. I also offered to e-mail her resume to my contacts database in an effort to get the word out that she was looking for a new job. In doing this for her, I expected nothing in return. She is a colleague and friend, as well as a hard worker, and I felt that any organization would be lucky to have her. The interesting thing is that while none of the job leads or connections I provided her panned out, she did find a new job as a project manager. Coincidently, her new employer was one of the companies I was targeting as an ideal client for my sales training program. A few weeks into her job, she sent me an e-mail asking how she might be able to help me make contact with the appropriate decision-maker at her company regarding sales training. She has since given me several contacts to help get the sales process started and continues to update me on the internal goings-on in case any of the internal activity might drive the need for sales training.

The bottom line is that when we help other people and don't expect anything in return, often we do get something in return. It may not be right away, it may not be ever, but many times at some point that person we helped will remember and want to help us when we have a need at some point in the future.

The other way to get fantastic referrals is to simply do a great job for your clients. Several months ago, a client of mine attended a Franklin Covey seminar. While talking with another participant sitting next to him named Steve who worked for a Fortune 100 commercial paper products company, Steve shared with my client that his company was beginning to explore outsourcing some of their training programs, including sales training. My client shared with Steve the terrific results his team had with The Blitz Experience. Steve asked my client for my contact info, and I've since given a Blitz presentation to his boss and received a verbal commitment to move forward!

Another fabulous networking technique is what I call "target prospecting" or "company-specific networking." Here's how it works. Create a spreadsheet of your top ten most desirable premium accounts. The headings across the top of each column should read as follows: company name, contact name, mailing address, e-mail address, phone number, and notes.

Next, complete as much of the information on the spreadsheet that you already have, company name being the most obvious, but also include information such as mailing address and phone number if you have it. Whatever information you don't have, leave blank. Okay, here's where it gets interesting.

Now, e-mail your best referral partners and contacts and attach the desired premium accounts spreadsheet you've just completed. Send the e-mail to one referral partner at a time, rather than an e-mail blast, to keep it more personal. The body of the e-mail you send to your contacts should read something like this:

> "Hi (referral partner name)! I'm on a quest for some new premium accounts, and I'm hoping you can help me.
>
> Attached you will find a spreadsheet of my top ten most desired accounts. I have completed the information I already have, and I am hoping you will have some additional information I am missing, such as the appropriate contact name at each company. I prefer to speak directly with (title of your decision-maker); however, I would greatly appreciate having the contact information of anyone you know inside each organization so I may get my foot in the door.
>
> In exchange for your help with this project, I would be happy to do the same for you. Thanks in advance for your help!"

You may also consider offering a Starbucks gift card of a nominal amount as a thank-you for any information provided by each of your referral partners.

Also, you will notice the offer at the end of the e-mail that you would be happy to do the same for each of your referral partners. By offering to reciprocate, you increase your chances for success in getting your spreadsheet back with some of the additional information you're missing. You'll be happy to know that the people who receive your e-mail will be thrilled to help because they understand the effectiveness of a networking strategy such as this and will be able to implement the same strategy with you and their other referral partners.

Once you've compiled the remaining information on the spreadsheet you were initially lacking, you now have the information you need to get your foot in the door with each of your premium accounts. Now, instead of cold calling, you should have a contact name at each company. If the contact at each desired premium account given by your referral partners is your typical decision-maker, great! All you have to do now is call the person to whom you've been referred and use the name of your referral partner as a reference.

If the person you have been referred to is not your typical decision-maker, you still have the "in" you need. Begin your search for your desired contact within each desired premium account by calling the contact you were given by your referral partner, using your referral partner's name as a reference. Next, simply ask the person you've been referred to who at their company would be the appropriate person for you to speak with based on the products and services you offer.

ACTIVITY:

Identify three prospects with whom you'd like to do business and reach out to your networking partners to determine who in your network knows someone at each prospect's company.

5

Leveraging Voicemail and E-Mail to Schedule Qualified Appointments

The key to leaving an effective voicemail message is: "Less is more." In other words, the shorter your voicemail message, the better, and the more likely you are to get a response from the prospect. The common mistake we as salespeople make is that we consider voicemail an opportunity to leave a three-minute commercial, rather than the more appropriate use of voicemail, to get the prospect to call us back.

Many times, we leave voicemail messages that are so detailed the prospects decide they are not interested and do not call us back. The better tactic is to leave a short, concise message that includes an element of curiosity so the prospect is intrigued and therefore has a reason to return the call.

For example, referring to a well-known company in the prospect's industry with whom you currently do business creates curiosity. Using this technique, my voicemail message might sound something like this:

> "Hi, Mr. Prospect. This is Andrea Sittig-Rolf with Sittig Incorporated. I'm calling about ABC Company. Will you please return my call at 206-769-4886? Thank you."

That's it, nothing more, hang up. Now, the strategy to this technique working successfully is in the way you handle the conversation when the prospect calls you back. To avoid the prospect feeling tricked into calling you back, here is how the return call should be handled:

Prospect: "Yes, I'm just returning your call about ABC Company."

Andrea: "Great! Thanks for calling me back. ABC Company is a client of ours for whom we have provided sales training services that have increased sales team production by 27 percent. Because you are in a similar industry, I thought we might be able to help your company in the same way. Are you available to meet next Thursday at 10:00 a.m. for about thirty minutes to discuss this further?"

By immediately referring back to ABC Company as the reason why you called, you avoid the prospect feeling deceived into returning your call, and you are immediately showing the connection between your client, ABC Company, and your prospect.

Another version of this voicemail that is a little more direct is the following:

"Hi, Mr. Prospect. This is Andrea Sittig-Rolf with Sittig Incorporated, creator of The Blitz Experience. I'm calling to tell you about some of the fantastic sales results we've created for companies such as ABC Bank and XYZ Software company. Will you please return my call at 206-769-4886? Thank you."

Speaking to the results you've created for other companies gives you credibility with news, and being brief in the voicemail message you leave creates curiosity, both of which will increase your chances of getting a return phone call.

Another technique that works well is to refer to another salesperson who is no longer with your company. Using this technique, my voicemail message might sound something like this:

"Hi, Mr. Prospect. This is Andrea Sittig-Rolf with Sittig Incorporated. I'm calling about Bob Smith. Will you please return my call at 206-769-4886? Thank you."

Again, the success in this technique is in the way the call is handled on the call back. Here is how the return call should go:

> **Prospect:** "Yes, I'm just returning your call about Bob Smith."

> **Andrea:** "Great! Thanks for calling me back. I see from our records that you were working with Bob, and he is no longer with our company. I just wanted to follow up to be sure you're being taken care of and to learn more about your company so I'm sure we can best serve you. Are you available next Thursday at 10:00 a.m. to meet for about thirty minutes?"

Again, immediately showing the connection between Bob Smith, the salesperson who is no longer with my company, and the prospect is crucial in the success of this technique.

An additional effective technique is to team up with another salesperson in your company and trade lists of prospects you have not had success in working with. Using this technique, my voicemail message might sound something like this:

> "Hi, Mr. Prospect. This is Andrea Sittig-Rolf with Sittig Incorporated. I'm calling about Jane Jones. Will you please return my call at 206-769-4886? Thank you."

The conversation on the return call should go something like this:

> **Prospect:** "Yes, I'm just returning your call about Jane Jones."

> **Andrea:** "Great! Thanks for calling me back. You had spoken with Jane from my company some time ago. The reason for my call is that we've had great success with ABC Company, and I wanted to meet with you for about thirty minutes to determine if our sales training programs would increase sales production for your company as well.

Are you available next Thursday at 10:00 a.m. to meet for about thirty minutes?"

Once again, showing the connection between Jane Jones, my teammate, and the prospect is critical to the success of this technique.

For those of you who are in the real estate business, here's a great voicemail script for you:

> "Hi, Mr. Prospect. This is (your name) with (your company name). I'm calling regarding your property located at (property address or building name). Please return my call at (your phone number). Thank you."

Again, the key is less is more. Don't leave too much detail. You want to create curiosity so the prospect has a reason to call you back.

For those of you in the financial industry calling on existing customers to sell additional products and services, try this:

> "Hi Mr. Customer. This is (your name) with (your company name). I'm calling regarding your account. Please return my call at (your phone number). Thank you."

If you're in the insurance business, this one's a keeper:

> "Hi Mr. Customer. This is (your name) with (your company). I'm calling regarding your insurance policy. Please return my call at (your phone number). Thank you."

The key to the success in the above scripts is to simply refer to something belonging to the prospect, i.e., their property, their account, their insurance policy. When you refer to something that is familiar to the prospect and don't leave any detail you do two things. First, you gain instant credibility by having knowledge of their property, account, or insurance policy. Two, by keeping your voicemail message vague; you create curiosity and give the prospect a reason to return your call.

One final technique that works well after you've already had your first meeting with the prospect goes something like this, should you need to leave a voicemail message:

> "Hi, Mr. Prospect. This is Andrea Sittig-Rolf with Sittig Incorporated. I have just a few more questions for you. Will you please return my call at your earliest convenience? I can be reached at 206-769-4886. Thank you."

The idea here is to let the prospect know you have more questions. This is much more effective than the traditional voicemail message we might leave for a prospect after a meeting, which might go something like this:

> "Hi, Mr. Prospect. This is Andrea Sittig-Rolf with Sittig Incorporated. I just wanted to give you a quick call to follow up on our meeting. Please feel free to give me a call if you have any questions. I can be reached at 206-769-4886. Thank you."

Do you see the difference? In the first example, I've asked the prospect to call me back because I have more questions for him. In the second example, I asked the prospect to call me if he had any questions. The reason the first example is so much more effective is that it implies there are some loose ends that need to be dealt with, whereas the second example asks the prospect to call back only if he has questions. If he doesn't have questions, and he most likely won't, there's no reason for him to call back.

Try these techniques the next time you have the opportunity to leave voicemail messages, and be ready to handle the plethora of return calls! For even more ideas on leaving effective voicemail messages that get a response, check out Stephan Schiffman's book *Cold Calling Techniques...That Really Work!* (5th Edition, Adams Media, 2003).

In addition to leveraging voicemail as a powerful tool when leaving messages for prospects, it can also be a powerful tool when leaving a greeting, also known as the outgoing message, on your own voicemail. While attending a client sales conference earlier this year, I had the privilege of participating in a workshop facilitated by Shawna Schuh entitled "Power

Tools to Build Your Business." During the workshop, she explained how to use voicemail as a "power tool" when recording your outgoing greeting by using the acronym VOICE, as follows:

V = Visual
Let your voice convey a feeling, some emotion so the caller pictures you in a positive way.
O = Optimistic
Be up and have a smile in your voice, be happy that someone called.
I = Interesting
Most voicemail messages are boring, mundane, and the same, so making yours different and interesting is a definite advantage.
C = Clever
Let the caller know you appreciate them, want to speak to them, and get them thinking.
E = Energetic
Conveying energy over the phone is the best way to make a positive impression so people will leave a message.

The idea with leaving an effective voicemail greeting or outgoing message is not to give your callers instructions on what to do once they've reached your voicemail. Voicemail has been around long enough now that we all know what to do! We don't have to be told, "I'm either away from my office or on the other line. Please leave a message at the sound of the tone and I'll get back to you as soon as I can." Duh! We know that, right? So by way of example, Shawna suggests the following:

1. "Hi! You've reached the office of Ted Buick. I'm happy you called, and I promise to get back to you today by 5:00."
Note: Only make a promise if you absolutely, positively intend to keep it always.

2. "Hello, this is Julie Mustang with the Road Runner Company. It's a pleasure to serve you, so expect a return call soon."

Note: Be sincere. If you dislike serving people, don't say you like it!

3. "Hi! You've reached the voice of Todd Chevrolet, which is as close to me as you'll come today. I will be returning calls on Thursday if you leave a message. Until then, you can call Julie at extension 202 for immediate service."
Note: There is no mention of where Todd is—no one cares!

4. "It's the voice of Buck Chrysler, and I think it's great that you called. Details are ideal, so leave me some and I'll get back to you soon."
Note: All of these examples were taken from the book *How to Nail Voice Mail* by Shawna Schuh, which you can order online at www.businessgraces.com.

In addition to leveraging voicemail as a powerful appointment-setting tool, an example of how e-mail is used as a powerful appointment-setting tool is as follows. Send an e-mail of introduction including something of value to the prospect that isn't necessarily selling the prospect, but rather is providing useful information that will help the prospect in their business. For instance, you may know something that's going on in the prospect's industry and could include an article or press release that offers pertinent information and then offer to meet in person to discuss what's going on in their industry.

Some other compelling topics of conversation include strategy discussions, marketplace discussions, and industry trends discussions. In other words, the reason for your meeting in person is to discuss these issues in general, which may be more appealing to your prospect. Then, when you're in front of your prospect face to face, you will have the opportunity to discuss the specifics of these topics and how your solution(s) may be relevant to their business initiatives.

Better yet, when you are referred to a new prospect, put the name of the person who referred you in the subject line of the e-mail. Assuming the person who has referred you is known by the prospect, you can guarantee your e-mail will be opened.

Another technique that works well is to send an e-mail as a follow-up after the initial meeting, and if the prospect doesn't respond within a week, send the **exact same e-mail** again one week after sending it the first time. Do not change a thing from your initial e-mail and do not reference that you've sent it before. The reason this works is that by sending the same e-mail more than once, it acts as a reminder to the prospect without insulting them by telling them, "Hey, I've sent this before and you still haven't responded!" You can keep track of the e-mails you send in Outlook either in a folder or as a "to do" on your calendar. Send the same initial follow-up e-mail you sent three times, one week apart. Usually by the second or third time you send it, you will get a response.

Also, try alternating leaving voicemail messages and sending e-mail so you give the prospect the option of either calling you back or sending an e-mail based on what's most convenient for them.

Now, there is a limit to how often to follow up and for what length of time to continue following up. If the prospect is completely unresponsive after you've sent the same e-mail three times and have left several voicemail messages over a period of a month or more, stop following up for now. If prospects ignore you after many attempts on your part, they are either not interested or something has happened in their business or personal life that is preventing them from getting back to you. It could also be that either they have made a decision to go with another solution, whether it be internal or with one of your competitors, or something in their business has changed that makes your product or service unnecessary.

Before giving up completely on the follow-through, I recommend doing two things:

- Wait two months between your last attempt and your next attempt. Sometimes after time has passed, it may be easier to reach the prospect. Things may have settled in either their personal or business life, if that in fact was the reason the prospect didn't get back to you initially. It could be that they still have a need for your product or service, but have simply forgotten about it since meeting with you.

- As a final attempt only, you can try a technique I call "the take-away." This technique leaves it up to the prospect to call you when they're ready to proceed. It goes something like this:

"Hi, Mr. Prospect. This is Andrea Sittig-Rolf with Sittig Incorporated. I've made several attempts to contact you since our first meeting and have not been able to reach you. I understand you are very busy and that you haven't had a chance to get back to me. I won't be contacting you again, so please feel free to contact me when you're ready to proceed with the solution we discussed. I can be reached at 206-769-4886. Thank you."

Now, I know what you're thinking...it's risky. Yes, it is. That's why it's designed to only be used as a final attempt. When you've reached the point where it's obvious to you that the prospect is no longer interested or has decided on another solution, try this technique as a last resort.

ACTIVITY:

Create a voicemail and e-mail script based on the techniques presented here.

6

The "Aha!" Formula

Anticipate the objection, Handle the objection, Ask for the appointment. The "Aha!" Formula works every time for securing qualified appointments with decision-makers. It sounds simple, and it is. But so often we're intimidated by the word "No," so rather than handle the objection or perceived rejection, we simply thank the prospect, hang up the phone, and make the next call. Imagine, though, having to make fewer prospecting phone calls because you have improved your appointment-setting skill level.

Before we get to the heart of this chapter, first we must consider getting past the gatekeeper so that once we have the decision-maker on the phone, we can use the "Aha!" Formula and the overcoming common objections techniques I describe. Here are some examples of how the conversation with the gatekeeper might sound:

> **Receptionist:** "ABC Company, how can I direct your call?"
> **Andrea:** "Hi. My name is Andrea Sittig Rolf, and I'm with Sittig Incorporated. I'd like to talk to your sales manager, please."
> **Receptionist:** "Can I tell him what this is regarding?"
> **Andrea:** "Sure. We are the developer and exclusive provider of a sales training program called The Blitz Experience, and I'd like to set up a time to meet with him to determine whether this program will be of benefit to ABC Company."
> **Receptionist:** "Is he expecting your call?"
> **Andrea:** "Well, no, not exactly."

Receptionist: "Hold, please."
Sales manager's voicemail: "Hi. I can't take your call right now, so please leave a message and I'll call you back as soon as possible."

Sound familiar? Ever get the feeling the receptionist has been trained just to screen your calls and keep you away from connecting with your prospect at her company? Well, guess what, she has!

Conversations like the above haunted me in the early years of my sales career. After dealing with this same conversation over and over again, I decided there must be a better way, so I started to experiment. Here's what I learned...

The receptionist can either make or break you in any organization. She holds the key to your success in terms of actually directing you to the person you want to talk to. I've said "her company" and "her organization" previously because as far as you are concerned, it is **her** company. (Or his company, if you're dealing with a male receptionist.) The point is that knowing this, there are a few things you can do.

First, engage the receptionist. Then, be genuine in your approach. Receptionists can smell a rat from hundreds of miles away; that's part of their training, too.

Many times, just by logging on to a company Web site, you can find the name of the chief executive officer or president of the company. Make note of this before making your call. Let's say the chief executive officer of the company you're calling is John Jones. Now, let's take a look at how the conversation with the receptionist should go:

Receptionist: "ABC Company, how can I direct your call?"
Andrea: "Hi. My name is Andrea Sittig-Rolf, and I'm with Sittig Incorporated. I'm hoping you can help me. I'm looking for the person in your organization who would make a decision regarding sales training. That wouldn't be John Jones, would it?"

> **Receptionist:** "Oh no, that wouldn't be John Jones. That would be Bob Smith."
> **Andrea:** "Great! Can I speak to Bob, please?"
> **Receptionist:** "Sure, I'll transfer you."
> **Andrea:** "Thank you."

Believe it or not, most of the time, this technique works and will get you to the person you need to talk to. The idea is that the receptionist doesn't want to bother John Jones, the chief executive officer, with a cold call from a salesperson. It's almost a relief for her to be able to transfer you to Bob Smith, someone below John Jones on the organizational chart at the company.

Even if you are unable to speak to Bob Smith during this particular phone call, at least now you have the name of the person you need to talk to for the next time you call. Receptionists don't screen calls as much when you have the name of the person you want to talk to.

On another note, I know it seems obvious, but for goodness sake, say "Please" and "Thank you!" You would not believe the salespeople I've trained who don't even say "Please" and "Thank you" when dealing with receptionists, or anyone else for that matter. Simple courtesy goes a long way.

In the situation where you are talking to someone other than the receptionist who you realize is not the decision-maker and they tell you, "I'm not the one to talk to regarding your products or services," do not say, "Oh, well who is?" Instead say, "Really? What is it you do?" and again, engage the person in conversation for a bit before asking who you should talk to instead.

Another tip is to avoid dealing with the gatekeeper at all and simply ask for the sales department immediately when the receptionist answers. Believe me, callers are not screened when calling on the sales department, for obvious reasons. Then, when you get a salesperson on the phone, say something like, "Hi. I'm not sure if you can help me, but I'm actually hoping to talk to your sales manager. Who would that be?" Salespeople are not trained to screen calls and they love to talk, so chances are you'll get plenty of information about the company you're calling on as well as the person you ultimately need to talk to.

Finally, when the receptionist answers, you can also try asking for the accounting or accounts receivable department. You won't get screened by the receptionist from those departments either, and people in those departments aren't trained to screen calls, so chances are, they'll give you the information you need!

Okay, now that you're past the gatekeeper and you have the chance to actually speak to the decision-maker, let's briefly look at your opening script when calling on a new prospect for the first time. The purpose of your phone call is to **get the appointment;** therefore, you should say so right up front. Also, the point of meeting with the prospect is not to tell them about how great you and your company are, but rather to learn about them and their company to better understand what solution you can provide. You should address this in your opening script, and it should go something like this:

> "Hi, Mr. Prospect. My name is Andrea Sittig-Rolf, and I'm the creator of The Blitz Experience, an activity-based sales training program that empowers salespeople to schedule appointments with qualified prospects the day of the training, resulting in a pipeline full of new opportunities at the end of the day. The reason for my call today is to schedule an appointment to learn more about your sales organization so we can determine whether there is a fit for The Blitz Experience within your firm. How's Thursday at 10:00 a.m. work for you?"

Your opening script should include a brief overview of who you are and what you do, and then get right to the point of setting the appointment. The reason for your call is to set the appointment, not to sell your solution. Avoid the temptation to answer a myriad of questions. Sometimes, prospects will engage you over the phone in an effort to avoid meeting with you in person, and by engaging in a long, drawn-out conversation, you may talk yourself right out of the appointment. Instead, stay focused and remember that your extended conversation should happen in person and not over the phone. Also, remember that the purpose of your appointment is to **learn more about the prospect and not to tell them all about you,** and it is important to convey this message during your opening script (i.e., "…The reason for my call today is to schedule an appointment to learn more about your organization so we can determine whether there is a fit for our solution. How's Thursday at 10:00 a.m. work for you?")

Before you can begin to share all the wonderful benefits of your company, you must first learn about your prospect to determine whether there is a fit between your prospect's needs and your solution. More about this will be covered later, but for now, I will explain how to overcome the most common objections and get the appointment by using the proven methodology of the "Aha!" Formula.

Okay, now that you're past the gatekeeper and you have had a chance to try your opening script with the prospect, here is when the "Aha!" Formula kicks in. Now, you may be saying to yourself, "Yeah, I get it. The 'Aha!' Formula makes sense, but how do I overcome the objection? What exactly do I say in response to the objection, and how do I handle it and then get the appointment anyway?" I'm so glad you asked!

As good as your opening script is, most of the time you will encounter objections from your prospect while setting the appointment. After years of conducting The Blitz Experience, as well as taking some good advice from Stephan Schiffman, author of a fantastic book on cold calling called *Cold Calling Techniques…That Really Work!* (5th edition, Adams Media, 2003), the most common objections you will hear fall into the ten categories below:

1. "No, thanks. I'm happy with what I have."
2. "I'm not interested."
3. "I'm too busy."
4. "Send me some literature."
5. "I once had a bad experience with your company."
6. "We don't have money to buy anything right now."
7. "What makes your company so good?" or "Why should I switch to you?"
8. "Just give me the thirty-second version of your presentation."

9. "We're not in the market right now."
10. "How much is it?"

As I mentioned in the "Aha!" Formula, the key is to anticipate and handle the objection properly before asking for the appointment, and always asking for the appointment after handling the objection. Keep in mind that you may hear more than one objection in any given phone call. In other words, the prospect may say, "I'm not interested," and after handling that objection you might hear, "I'm happy with what I've got," and then you might hear, "We don't have any money." Prospects may give multiple objections, some of them true, some of them false and just used as a tool to get you off the phone! While it's important not to take the first "No" for an answer, I don't recommend overcoming more than three objections in any given phone call. Sometimes, the answer is "No." However, by learning how to overcome the most common objections, you'll significantly increase your appointments ratio. In this chapter, I will give many examples of exactly how to overcome each of the most common objections you will hear when making phone calls to schedule appointments with qualified decision-makers.

"No, thanks. I'm happy with what I have." Also known as "status quo," this is probably the most difficult objection to overcome, because people don't want to change unless there is a compelling reason to do so. The key to handling this particular objection is to describe how your product or service **complements, enhances, or supplements** what the prospect is already doing. In other words, don't put yourself in the position of competing with the prospects current vendor, and possibly insulting the prospect's earlier decision to go with your competitor; instead, your solution will actually enhance what they're already doing. This works so well, because now the prospect doesn't have to choose one or the other, but can instead have both: The former decision they made regarding the same products and services you offer can simply be enhanced by what you provide. By using this technique, you're actually reinforcing what the prospect is already doing by showing that your solution will fit into their particular plan. You can also try the tactic of "We don't mind being second," which indicates your interest in having at least some of their business, if not all of it.

This tactic in overcoming the "I'm happy now" objection works well in my business of sales training. Often, the prospects I call on are already doing something in regards to sales training, but because of the specific appointment-setting techniques training I do, my Blitz Experience program often complements or reinforces other training programs the prospect might already have in place.

To understand the practicality of this technique, the example below demonstrates exactly how this technique can be used:

> **Andrea:** "Hi, Mr. Prospect. My name is Andrea Sittig-Rolf, and I'm the creator of The Blitz Experience, an activity-based sales training program that empowers salespeople to schedule appointments with qualified prospects the day of the training, resulting in a pipeline full of new opportunities at the end of the day. The reason for my call today is to schedule an appointment to learn more about your sales organization so we can determine whether there is a fit for The Blitz Experience within your firm. How's Thursday at 10:00 a.m. work for you?"
>
> **Prospect:** (Anticipate the objection.) "We're all set with sales training for the year. In fact, we just signed up for a program yesterday."
>
> **Andrea:** "That's great! May I ask what kind of program it is?"
>
> **Prospect:** "Sure, it's sales process training, and it's conducted by XYZ Company."
>
> **Andrea:** (Handle the objection.) "Well, that's perfect actually, because The Blitz Experience will enhance that program beautifully by focusing on the very first phase of the sales process; setting the appointment." (Ask for the appointment.) "Why don't I come by next Wednesday at 10:00 a.m. to learn more about your company and your new sales training program so we can determine whether The Blitz Experience will enhance what you're already doing?"
>
> **Prospect:** "Okay."

Notice the "Aha!" Formula used throughout the script. By anticipating the objection, I was ready to handle the objection and then ask for the appointment. Easy, right? It's actually not too bad when all you have to do is overcome one objection and then get the appointment. However, as I mentioned previously, sometimes prospects will give more than one objection. Using the same example above, the multiple objections script might go something like this:

> **Andrea:** "Hi, Mr. Prospect. My name is Andrea Sittig-Rolf, and I'm the creator of The Blitz Experience, an activity-based sales training program that empowers salespeople to schedule appointments with qualified prospects the day of the training, resulting in a pipeline full of new opportunities at the end of the day. The reason for my call today is to schedule an appointment to learn more about your sales organization so we can determine whether there is a fit for The Blitz Experience within your firm. How's Thursday at 10:00 a.m. work for you?"
>
> **Prospect:** (Anticipate the objection.) "We're all set with sales training for the year. In fact, we just signed up for a program yesterday."
>
> **Andrea:** "That's great! May I ask what kind of program it is?"
>
> **Prospect:** "Sure, it's sales process training, and it's conducted by XYZ Company."
>
> **Andrea:** (Handle the objection.) "Well, that's perfect actually, because The Blitz Experience will enhance that program beautifully by focusing on the very first phase of the sales process, setting the appointment." (Ask for the appointment.) "Why don't I come by next Wednesday at 10:00 a.m. to learn more about your company and your new sales training program so we can determine whether The Blitz Experience will enhance what you're already doing?"
>
> **Prospect:** (Anticipate the objection.) "Why don't you just send me some literature?"
>
> **Andrea:** (Handle the objection.) "I'd be happy to send you more information, and I have found it to be more

useful when it's targeted to your specific needs." (**Ask** for the appointment.) "Why don't I just come by Wednesday at 10:00 a.m. to learn more about your sales organization, and I'll bring plenty of literature with me?"
Prospect: "Okay."

In this scenario, if the prospect had given me one more objection, I would handle it and ask for the appointment for the last time. Beyond overcoming three objections in a row, your prospecting phone call turns into an argument, which is the last impression you want to leave with the prospect when hanging up the phone! After hearing three objections, simply thank the prospect, hang up, and make your next call.

Another way to handle the "I'm happy now" or "status quo" objection is as follows:

Prospect: (Anticipate the objection.) "We're all set."
Andrea: (Handle the objection.) "That's great! We actually don't mind being second, and we can offer alternative pricing to keep your primary vendor honest, or we may find out we offer something your primary vendor does not." (Ask for the appointment.) "Why don't we get together Tuesday at 9:00 a.m. so I can learn more about your existing solution and how we might work with what you already have?"

Let's move on to the next category, "I'm not interested," probably heard more often than any other objection when prospecting for appointments. The key here is to describe the **result** your solution provides and, more specifically, the result your solution has provided someone else (i.e., another customer). Here's what I say when I have **A**nticipated the objection and the prospect tells me he's not interested:

Andrea: (Handle the objection.) "You know, Mr. Prospect, that's what many of my customers said before they understood that The Blitz Experience would actually double the number of appointments with qualified prospects their salespeople were able to set as a result of the skills and techniques taught and practiced during the Blitz." (Ask for the appointment.) "Why don't I just come by at 3:00 p.m. next Tuesday so I can share with you some actual results other customers have enjoyed by participating in a Blitz Experience of their own?"

Notice here I explained a typical result my customers have had from The Blitz Experience. I said, "You know, Mr. Prospect, that's what many of my customers said before they understood that The Blitz Experience would actually double the number of appointments with qualified prospects their salespeople were able to set as a result of the skills and techniques taught and practiced during the Blitz." Offering a sales training program that can double the number of appointments typically set for a sales team is a compelling argument when talking to a new prospect for the first time. By immediately explaining a compelling result, I am more likely to get the appointment.

In addition to offering the general results that can be expected from The Blitz Experience, I might give a specific result that a named client or client industry has experienced. Using the same objection as above, here's what that conversation would look like:

> **Prospect:** (Anticipate the objection.) "I'm not interested."
> **Andrea:** (Handle the objection.) "You know, Mr. Prospect, that's exactly what ABC Bank said until they tried The Blitz Experience and closed over $10 million in sales as a direct result of the qualified appointments scheduled during the Blitz. They have since rolled out the Blitz program to their entire company!" (Ask for the appointment.) "Why don't I just come by at 10:00 a.m. next Wednesday so I can share with you some more incredible results other customers have enjoyed by participating in a Blitz Experience of their own?"

Next, the "I'm too busy" objection is also quite common. The beauty of this objection is that you don't want to talk to them now anyway; you want to set an appointment to talk in person! If they're too busy to talk, that's the very reason to set an appointment, so you can talk face to face when they're less busy and have scheduled you in their calendar. Another technique that works well here is if they're too busy to talk and they ask you to call back to schedule the appointment, suggest that you **tentatively** schedule an appointment now and that you'll call back to confirm. Microsoft conducted a study that showed there is a 70 percent greater chance an activity will happen if it's scheduled in the calendar. So, in our scenario, there is a 70 percent greater likelihood the prospect will honor the appointment and meet with you if you can get him or her to put it in their calendar. With multiple objections given on this particular call, it might go something like this:

> **Prospect:** (Anticipated objection.) "Andrea, you've caught me at a time when I'm too busy to talk."
>
> **Andrea:** (Handle the objection, Ask for the appointment.) "Okay, well then rather than taking time now, why don't I just come by next Thursday at 11:00 a.m.?"
>
> **Prospect:** (Anticipated objection.) "Well, why don't you call me back to schedule an appointment?"
>
> **Andrea:** (Handle the objection, Ask for the appointment.) "I'd be happy to, but why don't we go ahead and tentatively get it on the calendar now, and I'll call back to confirm?"
>
> **Prospect:** "Okay, what did you say? Next Thursday at 11:00 a.m.? See you then."

Even with up to three objections in one call, each should be Anticipated and Handled, and you should always Ask for the appointment. This is the "Aha!" Formula in action!

The next popular category of objection is "Send me some literature." I actually quite enjoy this objection, because I have a funny way to handle it. Feel free to use this one for those of you who are brave enough to do so! When the prospect has told me, "Send me some literature," I have Anticipated this objection and here's how I Handle it: "I'd be happy to send you some literature, but just so you know the package it comes in is five feet eight inches, 150 pounds, with dark hair (Ask for the appointment), and it'll be there Friday at 9:00 a.m.!" Obviously, the package I'm describing is myself and not an actual package, but it gets a laugh every time and gets the appointment most of the time! The point is to use humor when you can. Most people will appreciate it, and it will break the ice and give you leverage to actually getting the appointment.

On a more serious note, another way to handle the "Send me some literature" objection might go like this:

> **Andrea:** (Handle the objection.) "I'd be happy to send you some literature. However, until I learn more about your company and its needs, I won't know what to send." (**Ask** for the appointment.) "Why don't I come by at 2:00 p.m. on Thursday so I can learn more about your company and possible solutions we can provide so that I know what literature to share with you?"

This works well because, after all, you won't know what literature to send unless you find out more about your prospect and what their needs are, and how do you do that? You set an appointment!

Hopefully, the objection you will hear least often is, "I once had a bad experience with your company." If you hear this particular objection, the way to handle it is to first empathize with the prospect, then talk about how your company has **changed** since their bad experience. Now, if their bad experience was yesterday, you're in trouble because your company did not change overnight. However, if their bad experience was several years ago, chances are your company has changed since then, and that's the very reason you should meet, to remedy their bad experience and learn more about how you might do business with them now. Here's how this might sound:

> **Prospect:** (Anticipate the objection.) "We once had a bad experience with your company a few years back."
> **Andrea:** (Handle the objection.) "I'm sorry to hear that. You know we've actually changed quite a bit since then." (**Ask** for the appointment.) "Why don't I just come by next Thursday at 10 a.m. to learn more about your company and discuss how we've changed in a way that might be of benefit to you?"

Another reason the prospect may have had a bad experience with your company is that he or she was mistreated by the salesperson he or she was working with at the time. If that salesperson is no longer with your company, that is a perfect reason to meet, so you can make up for whatever the original salesperson did wrong at the time. Here's how that would go:

> **Prospect:** (Anticipate the objection.) "We worked with a salesperson from your firm years ago who did a terrible job for us."
> **Andrea:** (Handle the objection.) "I'm really sorry to hear that. That person is no longer with our company, which is exactly why we should meet." (Ask for the appointment.) "How does Friday at 2 p.m. work for you?"

Another common objection you might hear is, "We don't have money to buy anything right now" or "It's just not in the budget." During one of my Blitz Experience role-play exercises, I used the objection, "I don't have any money," with the salesperson. I loved his response. He said to me, "Well, neither do I. That's why I'm calling you!" He said he actually uses this technique and it works most of the time because he gets the prospect to laugh, thus letting his guard down, allowing the salesperson to get the appointment.

A more serious way to handle this objection might sound like this:

> **Prospect:** (Anticipate the objection.) "It's not in our budget right now."
> **Andrea:** (Handle the objection.) "In that case, now is the perfect time to meet, before you're even in the market for a program like ours so we can take our time to learn more about your organization and how our Blitz program will be of benefit." (Ask for the appointment.) "Why don't I just come by at 10:00 a.m. on Thursday so I can learn more about your sales team and share more about how our Blitz program has doubled the number of appointments a typical sales force will schedule in one day?"
> **Prospect:** "Okay, see you then."

Another way to handle the "We don't have any money" objection goes like this:

> **Prospect:** (Anticipate the objection.) "We don't have any money."
>
> **Andrea:** (Handle the objection.) "Actually, we have several payment plans that make our sales training programs quite affordable. Also, we've found that most clients sell upwards of $100,000 in products and services as a direct result of the appointments they schedule during the Blitz training." (Ask for the appointment.) "Why don't I come by next Tuesday at 2:00 p.m., and I'll share some of the amazing results our clients have had in participating in The Blitz Experience?"
>
> **Prospect:** "Okay."

With the "We have no money" objection, there are many ways you can go. You can discuss payment plans, leasing options, no money down, ninety-day payment, and other terms that may make your solution more appealing to your prospect. Your willingness to work with them and their budget will increase your chances of getting the appointment and ultimately getting the sale. Also, if you're able to show how your solution actually increases your client's profitability, you will be more likely to get the appointment and get the sale. Prospects aren't as impressed with you saving them money or making them more productive, because they've heard it all before. If you can prove your solution will increase their revenue or profitability, you'll have their attention.

Another situation you may run into with prospects is having them ask you, "What makes your company so good?" or "Why should I switch to you?" This is the prospect's way of getting you to give your entire pitch over the phone, making the appointment unnecessary. Don't get caught up in this scenario. Instead, it should go something like this.

> **Prospect:** (Anticipate the objection.) "What makes your company so good?"
>
> **Andrea:** (Handle the objection.) "I do! That's the very reason we should meet!" Or (Handle the objection.) "Lots

of things make us great! That's exactly why we should get together, so I can learn more about your company and determine a fit for our solution." (Ask for the appointment.) "How's Thursday at 11:00 a.m.?"

Or

Prospect: (Anticipate the objection.) "Why should I switch to you?"

Andrea: (Handle the objection.) "Well, there are many reasons, which is the very reason we should meet in person." (Ask for the appointment.) "How's Wednesday at 9 a.m.?"

Another trick prospects often use goes like this:

Prospect: (Anticipate the objection.) "Just give me the thirty-second version of your presentation."

Andrea: (Handle the objection.) "I would be doing a great disservice to you to try and do that, which is exactly why we should get together." (Ask for the appointment.) "How's Friday at noon for lunch?"

Another common objection you may hear is: "We're not in the market right now." Here's how this should go:

Prospect: (Anticipate the objection.) "We're not in the market right now."

Andrea: (Handle the objection.) "Great, because now is actually the best time to meet, before you're in the market, so you can take your time to learn about the best solution for your company and so I can help you determine the best solution based on your specific needs." (Ask for the appointment.) "How's Tuesday at 3:00 p.m.?"

Finally, another objection that sounds like a buying signal goes like this:

Prospect: (Anticipate the objection.) "How much is it?"

Andrea: (Handle the objection.) "We offer a variety of programs and solutions, and I'd be doing you a disservice to try and quote you a price over the phone." (Ask for the appointment.) "Why don't we just get together Thursday at 2:00 p.m. so I can learn more about your company and your needs to determine the appropriate investment?"

In a situation where you've already had your initial appointment and the prospect asks, "How much is it?" it truly is a buying signal. However, when making the initial phone call, it is usually a tactic used by prospects to get you off the phone, so don't be fooled!

When all else fails and you can't remember how to handle which objection, remember one technique I call "the conversation technique." I am blown away by how well this particular technique works. The key here is to handle the objection by asking an open-ended question (i.e., a question beginning with "Who," "What," "Why," "Where," "When," "How," or statements such as "Please describe," "Tell me about," or "Help me understand"). What this does is engage the prospect in conversation. Once the prospect is engaged, say, "You know, it sounds like we have a lot to talk about. Why don't I come by next Thursday at 9:00 a.m. to learn more about your business and determine how we might work together?"

In practicing this technique, something that commonly happens is the prospect will begin to ask you questions. The temptation by most salespeople is to answer all of the prospect's questions right then and there; after all, they must be interested if they're asking so many questions, right? Actually, what can happen is that you've answered all the questions that need to be answered and had an entire conversation about your products and services, so there's no need to set the appointment! You have literally talked yourself out of the appointment. Instead, the conversation technique teaches you to leverage the fact that you're having a conversation as the reason to meet in person. Let me give you an example of this technique:

> **Prospect:** (Anticipate the objection.) "We're not interested in sales training."
> **Andrea:** (Handle the objection by asking an open-ended question.) "Really? May I ask how you bring your

salespeople up to speed with your products and services and then teach them how to sell them?"

Prospect: "Our salespeople just work with their manager on a one-on-one coaching basis until the manager decides the salesperson is ready to go out on their own. What is the focus of your sales training program?"

Andrea: (Ask for the appointment.) "Our program focuses on the first phase of the sales process, getting the appointment. You know, it sounds like we have a lot to talk about. Why don't I come by Thursday at 10:00 a.m. so I can learn more about how your sales managers coach the salespeople to determine how our training might fit in with your existing process?"

Prospect: "Okay."

Using the same objection, here's another example using the open-ended phrase "Tell me about," which allows the prospect to elaborate on the hot buttons most important to him or her:

Prospect: (Anticipate the objection.) "We're not interested in sales training."

Andrea: (Handle the objection using the open-ended phrase "Tell me about.") "Okay. Will you please tell me about what you're doing now in terms of getting your salespeople up to speed to sell your products and services?"

Prospect: "Our salespeople just work with their manager on a one-on-one coaching basis until the manager decides the salesperson is ready to go out on their own. We've found sales training to be a waste of time and money, not having the ability to tie a direct positive result to the training seminars we've tried in the past."

Andrea: (Handle the objection.) "Yes, that's true of most sales training seminars out there. The difference with our program is that your salespeople are actually working during the training, prospecting for new business and scheduling appointments with real prospects, resulting in a pipeline full of new opportunities at the end of the day."

(Ask for the appointment.) "Why don't I swing by
Wednesday at 10:00 a.m., and I'll share with you some of
the positive, direct results other clients have had who have
participated in our Blitz Experience program?"
Prospect: "Okay."

By engaging the prospect in conversation, I now have the perfect reason to
meet in person. Remember that the key open-ended questions begin with
"Who," "What," "Where," "Why," "When," and "How," and the key open-
ended statements or phrases are "Tell me about," "Please describe," or
"Help me understand." Engage your prospect in conversation over the
phone, and use your conversation as the very reason to meet in person.

The point is that with all of these objections, use the "Aha!" Formula every
time to greatly increase your chances of getting the appointment and
starting the sales process with new prospects.

In addition to learning how to effectively overcome common objections, an
equally important lesson here is that you schedule an appointment or
appointments with yourself each week to make your appointment-setting
calls. Often, prospecting for new business is the activity that gets put on the
back burner when it's actually the most important in terms of keeping a full
pipeline of prospects. Scheduling this time with yourself will predict your
close ratio down the road, help you maintain sales consistency, and create
the habits that will guarantee your success as a sales professional.

While it is key to have the ability to overcome common objections and get
the appointment, there are also some things you can do to minimize hearing
objections in the first place. For example, using a creative mailer in advance
to get the prospect's attention and let him or her know you'll be calling
works well to reduce the likelihood of objections when you make your call.

I've practiced several effective strategies over the years that make the
appointment-setting call much easier, and I always get a positive response
from prospects.

First, send mail, unfolded, in a nine-by-twelve, brightly colored envelope
that matches your company colors. Handwrite the name and address of

your prospect on a company mailing label that includes your logo, and place it in the center of the envelope. Be sure to include enough postage, as the larger envelopes require more postage than the standard size envelopes.

Next, handwrite a message on the back flap of the envelope to get the prospect's attention, such as, "Referred by (referral source)" or "Information you requested enclosed" or "Information as promised" or "Looking forward to meeting you." Anything you can write on the back flap of the envelope that creates curiosity will inspire the prospect to actually open and read your materials.

Mail something bulky. For example, mail one baby shoe with your business card attached and write a note on the back of your card that says, "Just wanted to get my foot in the door," or something else that relates to your business. For example, I often mail a kazoo to prospects. One, it's a prop I use in my sales training programs, so it's directly relevant to my business. Two, it's bulky so it creates curiosity. And three, it immediately sends a message that my program is **fun**, an important part of my brand that is easily conveyed using this technique. Be sure to include a return address on the outside of the envelope so it's sure to be delivered by the post office.

Get the prospect's attention by sending the "skeleton mailer," to be used only as a last resort! I learned this one from Jerry Hocutt. When a prospect you have been trying to reach has not responded to your many voice messages, send a rubber skeleton in a nine-by-twelve, brightly colored envelope that matches your company colors. Attach a business card to the toe of the skeleton by punching a hole in the business card and tying it on the skeleton's toe with a short ribbon. On the back of the business card, write, "This is me, waiting for you, to call me back." Most people who have a sense of humor will respond to this, although you must choose carefully which prospects to send it to, based on the rapport you have with the prospect.

The last strategy to get a response is to mail items that are tactile in nature, in other words, something to feel and interact with, again using something that relates to your business. Again, the kazoo in my business works great, so think about something tactile that relates to your business that you could mail.

ACTIVITY:

Create a set of flashcards to help you overcome common objections. Index cards work fine for this exercise. Start by creating one card showing the "Aha!" Formula: **A**nticipate the objection, **H**andle the objection, **A**sk for the appointment. Keep this card in view at all times when making your appointment-setting phone calls. Next, write each of the ten objection categories on an index card, and on the back of each index card, write your response, exactly how you would say it, based on the techniques you've learned here. You should have one index card per objection category (i.e., one for "I'm happy now," one for "I'm not interested," one for "I'm too busy," and so on. Remember to include a couple of responses to each objection. (If you are participating in a Sittig Incorporated Blitz Experience, flashcards will be provided for you.)

7

Tracking Your Numbers, Knowing Your Numbers

(Visit www.sittiginc.com/files/SalesRepRadioMarch2006.mp3 to hear an eight-minute interview with Andrea Sittig-Rolf on SalesRepRadio To-Go regarding the importance of tracking and knowing your numbers.)

The key to any successful salesperson is the ability to predict with certainty the chances for success. Sales, therefore, is arguably a science. The seventh key, therefore, is that as a sales professional, you should know your personal sales numbers in order to predict with 100 percent accuracy your likelihood of reaching quota, as well as determining your income, based on consistently doing the numbers that will bring you success.

An excellent way to measure your results from appointment-setting calls is to keep a record of your calls and track your success. For example, I have created a form called "The Call Ratios Tracking Worksheet" (see Appendix C) that tracks calls, connects, appointments, voicemails, returned calls, proposals, sales, and even "Nos." A Call Ratios Tracking Worksheet template is also available for purchase at www.sittiginc.com in the "Shop Here" section, "Sales Secrets Downloads," should you wish to use a full-sized worksheet.

Take a look at the Call Ratios Tracking Worksheet in Appendix C, and I'll explain each section.

Each row going across the page represents one hour of calls and is separated by a space in between each row. In the margin of the worksheet, write the time of day you are making your calls next to each row. This will track what time of day is best to make your prospecting calls based on how often you're able to connect with your prospects.

Each column going down the page represents a different activity or outcome as you make your prospect calls (i.e., calls, connects, appointments, voicemails, returned calls, proposals, sales, "Nos"). As you make your calls, complete the worksheet based on the parameters below.

Calls

Calls are defined as each time you dial the phone, whether you reach anyone or not; if you've dialed, you count it as a "call" on your form. (If your focus is that of outside sales, the purpose of tracking your outbound calls is to determine your **pro-active, outbound activities** as they relate to sales. If the main focus of your job requires that you handle **incoming** calls, you can also use this form to track the inbound calls you receive.)

Connects

Connects are defined as actually talking to the decision-maker. Leaving a voicemail message does not count unless the decision-maker calls you back and you actually have a conversation, in which case it then counts as a connect. Also, leaving messages with receptionists or assistants doesn't count as a connect either.

Appointments

This section is pretty self-explanatory: When you schedule an appointment, you complete a bubble in the appointments section.

Voicemail

Here you will complete a bubble for each voicemail message you leave for a prospect.

Returned Calls

In this section, complete a bubble for each returned call you receive either as a result of leaving a voicemail message or leaving a message with the receptionist. Complete a bubble in the section of the worksheet that represents the time of day the call was returned. So, for example, if you leave a voicemail message in the morning during the first hour of calls, represented by the first row of bubbles across the top of the worksheet, and you receive a call back in the afternoon as a result of a voicemail message you left in the morning, you will complete the returned call bubble in the row that represents the time of day the call was returned.

Proposals

In this section, you complete a bubble when you've had the opportunity to propose your solution or quote a price on your product or service.

Sales

And of course, when you make a sale, you complete a bubble in this section.

Nos

You should also consider tracking the number of times you hear "No" when making your calls. Why on earth would you want to track every time you hear the word "No" from a prospect? Well, believe it or not, counting the "Nos" is equally important as counting your sales! How else will you know how often you typically hear "No" before you hear "Yes"? Hearing "No" is a very real part of the selling process, so it's important to know your personal "no ratio" so you can realistically plan your cold calling activities each week.

After tracking your calls for ninety days, add up the columns from each worksheet to understand your daily ratios, then add those up to understand your weekly call ratios, monthly ratios, ninety-day ratios, and so on. In ninety days, you should have a pretty good idea of your personal ratios. While this data will show you what your numbers are based on your current skill level (and simply by increasing the number of outbound calls you make, you can improve your sales ratio), you can also improve your **skill level** when making your calls, such as using the "Aha!" Formula for overcoming common objections as described in chapter six, and leaving effective voicemail and e-mail messages that get a response as described in chapter five. As your skill level improves, you will need to make fewer calls to achieve the same sales results, or continue to make the same number of calls for even greater sales results.

ACTIVITY:

Copy the Call Ratios Tracking Worksheet from Appendix C, purchase the template online at www.sittiginc.com, or create your own Call Ratios Tracking Worksheet. Based on the time of day you've shown to be the best for connecting with decision-makers, schedule an appointment with yourself each week and begin tracking your prospecting calls. Or, if you prefer to make daily prospecting calls, commit to making five connects a day with new decision-makers during the best time of day to reach them based on the personal data you've collected by completing the Call Ratios Tracking Worksheet.

Appendix A: Sales Training Programs, Keynotes, Workshops, and Books Offered by Sittig Incorporated

Sales Training Programs

Sittig Incorporated is the developer of an activity-based sales training program called The Blitz Experience that helps salespeople become more effective when prospecting over the phone. This unique sales training program requires prospecting activity the day of the training so sales reps are actually filling their pipelines with new opportunities using the techniques taught during the training. Blitz Experience clients have reported increased sales of as much as 20 percent as a direct result of this innovative sales training program. Here is what Sittig Incorporated clients have to say about The Blitz Experience:

> *"Since our Blitz Experience sales training program, we have gone from 23 percent of plan to 105 percent of plan! Our sales reps have changed their behavior to include consistent, proactive selling activities that have resulted in tremendous revenue growth for our company."*
> – Vice president of sales, telecommunications company

> *"Andrea, what a truly wonderful day! It was amazing to actually see the transformation of some of the reps' increased enthusiasm and energy. It was most definitely a day well spent. Thanks again for all of your support!"*
> – Sales manager, commercial furniture company

Sittig Incorporated also offers a sales training program based on Ms. Sittig-Rolf's first book, *Business-to-Business Prospecting: Innovative Techniques to Get Your Foot in the Door with Any Prospect* (Aspatore, 2005). This program includes exercises and activities that reinforce the strategies and techniques. Here are just a few comments from salespeople who have taken this class:

> *"The B2B Prospecting workshop was a valuable use of my time, because it brought to consciousness the fact that I need to primarily re-identify my current customer base and slowly adapt it to the ICP (ideal client profile) philosophy. Having us do homework ahead of time helped us to gain an understanding of your philosophies in*

advance so we could relax and get right to the meat of it at the workshop. You created a good/safe environment for all to participate."
– Project manager, interior construction services firm

"I learned the use of many different ideas for getting someone's attention at the B2B Prospecting Workshop that I will continue to use in my daily prospecting activities."
– Sales manager, commercial office furniture firm

"Andrea, your enthusiasm for the techniques and your positive attitude was infectious. It was very interesting to learn what people now thought their ICP (ideal client profile) was as opposed to prior to your training. You obviously have a ton of knowledge/success in B2B prospecting. I think this helped get "buy-in" from the group. You are very outgoing and got your techniques across successfully. I enjoyed the experience. Thanks!"
– Director of operations, business office interiors firm

To learn more about these sales training programs, contact Sittig Incorporated at 206-769-4886, info@sittiginc.com, or visit www.sittiginc.com.

Keynotes

Ms. Sittig-Rolf delivers informative and entertaining keynote speeches on sales-related topics at sales conferences and corporate events as well as association meetings. Choose from a variety of prepared keynotes, or have one customized especially for your event. Her animated and conversational style will engage your group immediately and will keep them learning and laughing throughout the presentation. Attendees of Ms. Sittig-Rolf's keynotes have said the following:

"Andrea, I wanted to say a big thanks for the great presentation you gave this morning! My colleague and I really enjoyed it and found your comments (and enthusiasm) extremely helpful!"
– Strategic administration specialist, Northwest
Agricultural Products

"Andrea, just wanted to say 'Thanks' for the presentation on Tuesday. Your attention-getting ideas will be most helpful. I'm looking forward to reading your book... I just skimmed the section on proposals and know there are ideas to make our proposals sizzle!"
– President, graphics design company

To learn more about the keynote offerings, contact Sittig Incorporated at 206-769-4886, info@sittiginc.com, or visit www.sittiginc.com.

Workshops

While Ms. Sittig-Rolf's keynotes address the **why**, her workshops address the **how**. Again, you may choose from a variety of prepared workshops on various sales-related topics, or have one customized for your group. Workbooks are provided, and your team will walk away with some effective sales tools to implement on real prospects and customers long after the workshop is over. Participants in Ms. Sittig-Rolf's workshops have had this to say:

"Andrea, thank you for your help with using marketing materials that get the prospects' attention. During your talk at the Columbia Tower Club, you shared the final puzzle piece that was missing; the clear envelopes. I'm now using this great idea of yours, and it has made all the difference!"
– Chief executive officer, high-end retail shop, Seattle

"Thanks again, Andrea, for the meeting this morning! (I'd blow my horn, but it's just not the same thru e-mail!) I've been reading your articles in the Puget Sound Business Journal, *and it was great to 'meet the real thing.' Your articles on "Use a well-written sales proposal" and "How to effectively follow-up after a first meeting" plus several others I've clipped and saved were not only well written but provided new info. There was some good take-away info this morning. Again, thanks and good luck to you and your business!"*
– Sales and marketing specialist, *Journal of Business*

To learn more about these workshops, contact Sittig Incorporated at 206-769-4886, info@sittiginc.com, or visit www.sittiginc.com.

Books

Ms. Sittig-Rolf is the author of *Business-to-Business Prospecting: Innovative Techniques to Get Your Foot in the Door with Any Prospect* (Aspatore Books, 2005), endorsed by best-selling author and sales guru Brian Tracy as well as Skip Miller, Steve Farber, and Ronald J. Walsh. It is available on Amazon.com and at Barnes & Noble bookstores. The following is what people are saying about her first book:

> *"This book shows you how to attract more and better customers, faster and easier than ever before."*
> – Brian Tracy, best-selling author and president, Brian Tracy International

> *"The first chapter on identifying your ideal client is worth the price of the book. Andrea convinced me. She clearly explains the huge bottom-line effect from not spending time chasing less-than-ideal clients added to the cumulative increase in business resulting from pursuing the right clients. This book offers great value to anyone in sales, marketing, management, and/or business ownership. The ideas are clearly stated and easy to implement. Andrea uses her own business in examples and explanations in the book. This is an easy read, which I enjoyed. Many business books are not. From identifying clients to winning proposals, Andrea sets out, step-by-step, how to build relationships that will result in sales and business growth."*
> – Amazon.com review, DEN, Seattle, Washington

> *"Clearly written and concise, the book lays out a solid framework with substance for performing business-to-business prospecting. Contains solid examples of how to apply techniques, greatly helping solidify the concepts. A solid read and highly recommended for any professional in business development."*
> – Amazon.com review, Bryan Minor, Bothell, Washington

Appendix B: Free Sittig Incorporated Sales Resources

SalesRepRadio To-Go Eight-Minute Interview: Maintaining Sales Consistency
www.sittiginc.com/files/SalesRepRadioMarch2006.mp3

Archived Webinar—Cold Calling: Getting Successful Sales Results (fifty-two minutes in length)
www.maximizer.com/productinfo/wmv/easeries_coldcalling.html

Free Sales Tips Newsletter
www.sittiginc.com/newsletter.cfm

Appendix C: Call Ratios Tracking Worksheet

Call Ratios Tracking Worksheet
APPOINTMENTS

CALLS	CONNECTS	APPOINTMENTS	VOICEMAIL	RETURNED CALLS	NOs	PROPOSALS	SALES	$ VALUE
OOOOO	OOOOO	OOOOO	OOOOO	OOOOO	OOOOO	OOOOO	OOOOO	
OOOOO	OOOOO	OOOOO	OOOOO	OOOOO	OOOOO			
OOOOO	OOOOO							
OOOOO	OOOOO							
OOOOO	OOOOO							
OOOOO	OOOOO	OOOOO	OOOOO	OOOOO	OOOOO	OOOOO	OOOOO	
OOOOO	OOOOO	OOOOO	OOOOO	OOOOO	OOOOO			
OOOOO	OOOOO							
OOOOO	OOOOO							
OOOOO	OOOOO							
OOOOO	OOOOO	OOOOO	OOOOO	OOOOO	OOOOO	OOOOO	OOOOO	
OOOOO	OOOOO	OOOOO	OOOOO	OOOOO	OOOOO			
OOOOO	OOOOO							
OOOOO	OOOOO							
OOOOO	OOOOO							
OOOOO	OOOOO	OOOOO	OOOOO	OOOOO	OOOOO	OOOOO	OOOOO	
OOOOO	OOOOO	OOOOO	OOOOO	OOOOO	OOOOO			
OOOOO	OOOOO							
OOOOO	OOOOO							
OOOOO	OOOOO							
OOOOO	OOOOO	OOOOO	OOOOO	OOOOO	OOOOO	OOOOO	OOOOO	
OOOOO	OOOOO	OOOOO	OOOOO	OOOOO	OOOOO			
OOOOO	OOOOO							
OOOOO	OOOOO							
OOOOO	OOOOO							

TOTAL_____ TOTAL_____ TOTAL_____ TOTAL_____ TOTAL_____ TOTAL_____ TOTAL_____ TOTAL_____ $

About the Author

Andrea Sittig-Rolf helps sales organizations inspire change, maximize sales, and increase bottom-line results. Business savvy with a passion for people, she understands how to help salespeople be their best and has what it takes to inspire them. She is a successful entrepreneur, author, and sales trainer, and is in high demand as a speaker and workshop leader.

Ms. Sittig Rolf is the author of a compelling sales book called *Business-to-Business Prospecting: Innovative Techniques to Get Your Foot in the Door with any Prospect* (Aspatore Books, 2005) endorsed by best-selling author and leading sales guru Brian Tracy, as well as leading sales professional authors Skip Miller, Steve Farber, and Ronald J. Walsh. She is also the creator and exclusive writer of the column entitled "Sales Solutions," featured biweekly in *The Puget Sound Business Journal*, and a contributing writer to SellingPower.com's "One Minute Tip," featured daily on the SellingPower.com Web site.

She is a regular contributor to SalesRepRadio To-Go, a monthly audio magazine designed exclusively for sales reps and sales managers. Available on CD or instant MP3 download, it's loaded with timely sales advice from North America's top sales training professionals.

Ms. Sittig-Rolf is the founder and president of Sittig Incorporated, a sales training and consulting organization based in Redmond, Washington, found online at www.sittiginc.com. She is also the developer of The Blitz Experience, an activity-based sales training program designed to help salespeople become more effective when prospecting over the phone. The Blitz Experience is unique because it requires salespeople to practice what they learn the day of the training by scheduling appointments with real prospects, resulting in new business opportunities at the end of the day.

Andrea graduated from Southwest Texas State University in 1991 with a bachelor's degree in psychology. She lives in Redmond, Washington, with her husband, Brian.